What Others Are Saying About John, Barbara and

Outrageous Grace

Winner, Best New Non-Fiction Book,
Indie Awards
Finalist, Best Book Awards,
USA Book News
Winner, Michigan Notable Book Award

'A love story in more ways than one. Facing the future without trepi-
dation is one of life's greatest gifts . . . It leaves you limp, exhausted . . .
if it doesn't sell, there is no adventure left in literature.'

   Judd Arnett, Detroit Free Press

'On the blue Atlantic and in bleak hospital wards, John Otterbacher
has weathered the sorts of storms that ultimately define a person . . .
assuming they manage to survive. Otterbacher's gifts were his family
and friends, and the dream that sustained him. Ours is this book that,
with humour and humility, tells his tale.'

   Herb McCor

'This gripping story personifies the best Irish characteristics of determination, fortitude and, of course, humour . . . A wonderful and
inspiring story that you can't put down.'
    Jean Kennedy Smith, former Ambassador to Ireland

'Read it, and you will be carried away, living each suspenseful
moment with this remarkable family. Once I started this book I
could not stop! Dr John Otterbacher is a gifted story writer and a
man who truly emanates hope from his heart.'
    Rich DeVos, cofounder of Amway

'Anyone who appreciates the power of the ocean and the humility of
putting to sea in a sailboat will understand John and Barb's choice to
go to sea with his damaged heart. Anyone who doesn't, will, after
reading *Outrageous Grace*.'
    Elaine Lembo, *Cruising World Magazine*

'It is nothing less than a story about our capacity as humans to
imagine, perform, and soar. And, not unlike the inexorable pull of
the oceans themselves, *Outrageous Grace* is also a daring blueprint
that might force you to re-examine what you do, why you do it, and
what you are waiting for . . . a powerful elixir for anyone tiptoeing
through life and settling for dreams deferred.'
    Tom Rademacher, Grand Rapids Press

'I read *Outrageous Grace* last night. I read it in one sitting. I did not
plan it that way. I just could not put it down. It is extraordinary, so
rich in imagery . . . It is poetry.'
    Christine St John

'When hope and heart disease collide, hope sometimes wins.'
    Richard McNamara MD, Chief of Cardiology

'Wise people have known forever that life is a near death experience.
The costumes of our lives can be suffocating, and Otterbacher and
his family shed theirs going to sea . . . They win big and we win along
with them through their engrossing and perilous adventure story.'
    Jim Harrison, Author/Poet

Outrageous Grace

Taking the Long Way Home

John Otterbacher

ADLARD COLES NAUTICAL
LONDON

This edition published by Adlard Coles Nautical
an imprint of A & C Black Publishers Ltd
36 Soho Square, London WID 3QY
www.adlardcoles.com

Pencil sketch of *Grace* by Ann Thompson. Photo of *Grace* by Roland Adam.
Cruising World and *Sailing* Magazines for stories incorporated into the book.

First published as *Sailing Grace* in the United States by Samadhi Press

ISBN 978-1-4081-1278-6

A CIP catalogue record for this book is available from the British Library.

This book is produced using paper that is made from wood grown
in managed, sustainable forests. It is natural, renewable and recyclable.
The logging and manufacturing processes conform to the environmental
regulations of the country of origin.

Typeset in 11.25/14.5 Tibere-Light by Palimpsest Book Production Limited,
Grangemouth, Stirlingshire
Printed and bound in Great Britain by
Cox & Wyman

Further information can be found at www.sailing-grace.com

To Barbara, John Ryan, Katie and Erin
who lived the story before I wrote it down.

'Live all you can; it's a mistake not to. It doesn't so much matter what you do in particular, so long as you have your life. If you haven't had that, what have you had?'

HENRY JAMES
The Ambassadors

Contents

Foreword by

Paul Gelder, Editor _Yachting Monthly_

NO WONDER JOHN OTTERBACHER named his first yacht _Outrageous_. When he planned a year's sabbatical to go sailing with his wife, Barbara, he knew nothing about sailing, didn't have a boat and wondered if he could afford one.

Saving money for his dream, the family's new mantra became: 'Do we need it?' instead of 'Do we want it?' They found life more intense when they spent less. Instead of buying themselves out of trouble, they became proficient problem solvers.

John learned to sail not by the book, but from his own mistakes. 'Have you ever seen a spinnaker up sideways?' he asks. He bought lifelines and harnesses to keep the crew on deck, a sea anchor to slow the yacht down if they encountered a serious storm and, just in case it didn't, a reconditioned liferaft. Presciently, his son John Ryan announced: 'Dad, this boat is our destiny!'

The 'ultimate storm' turned out to be nothing to do with threatening weather but everything to do with survival. Having learned enough about sailing to make a single-handed Atlantic crossing, John discovered a ticking time bomb in his chest – a serious heart condition which threatened his grand plan for a circumnavigation in his second boat, *Grace*, again presciently named. For John certainly displayed amazing grace under extraordinary pressure. Some readers might pause to think 'There but for the grace of God go I' and then ask themselves 'How would I cope?'

There are so many metaphors in the sailing world that cross over to life on shore – rite of passage, crossing the bar, plumbing the depths. John met them all on a surgeon's operating table. Failed open-heart surgery left his cardiologist shaking his head in doubt, if not despair. But sailors are a resourceful, single-minded band of brothers. There's no hard shoulder to stop on at sea when disaster strikes. You must make the best of things.

'If I let pain run my life, I'll end up a cripple,' John resolved. 'There's no room for heart failure in a life this full.'

For him, sailing was an escape, a challenge and a therapy, all rolled into one big adventure in a small boat on a big ocean. John's intimate and poignant confession of how he defied medical odds and battled on with a gimpy heart is compelling, eloquent and, above all, inspirational.

The first time I met John, on board *Grace* at St Katharine's Dock in London, in the summer of 2001, I was struck by something indefinable. Was it his firm handshake? The special glint in his eye? Something in his Irish genes? There was certainly something of the poet about his descriptive writing on the oceans and his long voyages.

It wasn't till later that I realised what marks John out from the crowd. It's the fact that he has been to the brink and come back.

Introduction

WE MAKE OUR WAY TO THE SEA by different routes. Some
are born to it, raised from an early age entirely under a
saline or freshwater spell. Early and generally positive asso-
ciations, adventures with a parent of seemingly god-like
skill and command, are layered-up like fibreglass on a hull.
Sailors sprung of this familial strain are imbued with
legends and lore: the champions – the barriers broken,
charting the uncharted – the great and horrible storms.
These lucky ones often know the names and intricacies of
everything nautical, actually know what they are doing
when they loosen the docklines and cast off.

I have the deepest respect for those who possess
passed–down disciplines and competencies. I am not one
of them.

I grew up in a Midwestern working class American
family with no ostensible connection to the sea. My father,
a child of the Great Depression, shackled himself to a
theatre manager's job at an early age – 'Just happy to have
a job' he would say – and stayed with it doggedly until the
day he retired. My mother was a teacher, secondary at first
and sixth grader later, on either side of a long stint as a
stay-at-home mother. Our lives were centred in a neigh-

bourhood of like-minded people with parochial goals and regimes: work hard, talk straight, respect others, and be 'realistic' about the range of possibilities available to you.

Solid stock: diligent, practical, reliable and sound. Not a sailor among them.

What we did have on that one day a week when my father didn't march off to the theatre was 'the big lake'. Whatever restraint my parents normally placed on their range of aspiration, they shared a boundless enthusiasm for Lake Michigan, a one hour jaunt from our home in Grand Rapids, Michigan. Come Thursday we almost religiously filed out to our trusty Nash Rambler, piled in with the beach blankets and picnic baskets, and headed out to 'the lake'. And though we didn't fully appreciate it then, Lake Michigan more than deserved its place in the constellation of Great Lakes.

Only later would I learn that these five inland seas with their 244 million square kilometres of water surface and depths up to 400 metres contained a full 20% of the world's fresh water. Enough – if spread evenly – to cover the entire continental United States to a depth of three metres.

Later still, a fascination with heavy weather infused me with a sea captain's respect for Great Lakes violence: sudden-onset storms and mayhem, a thousand wrecks gaping up from uneven sandy floors.

What I knew in those sun-drenched early days was that if I paddled fast on my inflatable air mattress, stopping when my parents looked up from whatever they were doing, I could soon get out far enough to pretend not to hear my father's summons, pacing back and forth on the now distant shore.

I am seven, I am nine, I am free at last, out beyond the constraints and confines of life on land. I am on my own for a while, captain of my own small boat, the sky a northern blue above me, the soothing undulation of offshore waves, the breeze-softened caress of 29°C. I paddle out further when my father retreats round-shouldered up the beach to his towel, two-armed backstrokes up and over the waves, then stop as he turns back towards me, hand to his forehead to shield his eyes from the glare, my fingers trailing alongside in the cool water.

I am a hundred metres from shore now, an entirely free man, a seaman, alone in this sweetwater world. At some deep level perhaps, totally unplumbed by me, the hook is already set.

Years pass, decades, an early marriage, professional degrees, some college teaching, terms in the Michigan House of Representatives and Senate, a son, a private practice, and I am forty – entirely land-locked, never a day at sea. A playful conversation with Barbara after work leads to a spontaneous decision to 'work hard for five years, then take a year off'.

Barbara's smiling 'What do we do with the year?' yields an unpremeditated suggestion that we do a motorcycle tour of Europe and Africa.

'Are you ready to put John Ryan – he'll be thirteen then – behind the handlebars?' elicits an equally quixotic, 'How about going sailing?'

That I have never been sailing, that we have no boat and little money, gets dismissed with the wave of the hand and a bravado-laden 'We have five years to get ready.'

And we do.

Prologue

No longer disguised by darkness, the storm shrieks in the shrouds and around us, whipping the Atlantic into unforgiving turmoil.

'Another five knots,' Barbara squints up from the wind indicator. And when I say nothing, 'What can I get you?'

'I'm fine. Are the kids okay?'

'They're just stirring. Got a good night's sleep.'

'Like us,' a weary smile.

We stand silently for a while, surveying the agitated seascape. Our eyes meet. There is nothing to say. We both know. A big wind and growing, big seas and growing.

Barbara starts down the companionway, then stops and glances back, her brown eyes full of resolve. She will shepherd the girls through whatever comes.

The swells come at us as tall as houses, but long, like North Sea dikes, above us now, foam-capped but rarely breaking. Grace rises to meet them, over the top, then plunges down into the trailing trough where another one churns in, icy fingers reaching from its crest.

Flying fish, flushed out by Grace's hull, soar into the looming waveface, glancing off, arching over backwards, or fluttering up over the crest. We follow them up and over, another trough, another dark wave face.

This will be a long day; a day of attrition.

Above the ocean's angry face, the sky is a shocking blue. Mare's tails run from one jagged horizon to the other. The sun fails to burn the intensity out of the wind, which eats the sunlight whole and races on, invigorated. As Grace *soars over a swell, the rigging shudders with the snap and strain of the miniature staysail, then falls strangely silent in the ensuing trough, the sheer height of the next swell providing a moment's relief from the onslaught of wind.*

Damn, it's beautiful.

'We're making good time,' I assure Barbara, when she offers up an early lunch.

'Are we going too fast?' Her grasp tightens on the companionway slats, fingernails white with compression.

'I think we're okay.'

Wave-flattening gusts come on at noon, bending Grace *over further still. She plunges on gamely, a low groan down in her body from the harsh pounding. Her hull forges counter-waves as she passes, spray blowing back at me from their collisions with the oncoming swells.* This is what you are made for, *I remind the two of us.*

The wind stiffens in the early afternoon, seamless now, cold and merciless. This morning's blue hardens, a steel undulation beneath a steely sky. The swells continue to build, frothy and tumbling, row upon row, unrelenting. An occasional odd-angle renegade mounts a wave or is mounted, surging up to double the height of the others, and breaks in a hissing cascade.

A big one catches me by surprise, rearing up beside us – I've got you now *– and dropping like a load of wet cement. I go down with the impact, salt water burning my eyes, choking and spitting, but drag myself back up, yanking the wheel to centre.*

Grace *struggles to right herself, but is still sideways to the next breaking wave, a gunshot collision with the hull, sending her over again in the trailing effervescence. I lurch to the surface in a cockpit full of water, first blood on the knuckles of the hand gripping the wheel.*

I jerk the wheel to the left in the canyon between waves, and Grace *swings upright again, rising like a carnival ride over the third wave.*

A shouted consultation with Barbara: nothing broken above or below. Whatever the mayhem out here, she and the girls are secure.

Looking for reassurance, I tug at the harness line that tethers me to the toerail. Then I swing Grace *directly downwind, hoping to rob the swells of their momentum. I slacken the staysail as we turn, wringing some force out of the wind.*

Grace *is a 50-foot surfboard now. The oncoming wave lifts us from behind, carries us along on its back, and thrusts us into the trough ahead. The exhausted wave rumbles on under us as we skid along in the sizzling foam.*

The next wave lumbers in. We are plunging again.

●●●●●

Hours later, the sky black now, the cold comes to get me.

'Are you okay?' Barbara asks, in between regular ministrations of soup and hot chocolate, a grilled cheese sandwich, and the still shrill wind.

'I'll be fine,' I tell her. In reality I am not fine. I am shivering intermittently. Pressure is building in the centre of my chest.

Not now. I fumble for the bottle of nitro in my pocket.

This is the storm within the storm.

Death

'I did not care what it was all about.
All I wanted to know was how to live it.
Maybe if you found out how to live in it
you learned from that what it was all about.'

– Jake Barnes in Ernest Hemingway's *The Sun Also Rises*

LIKE THAT MOST DANGEROUS wave in a great storm, death breaks over you from an odd angle. During a Michigan October she arrives disguised as a lung infection: a nasty, unyielding response to an afternoon of sanding inside the fibreglass hull of our sailboat, *Grace*.

'That stuff's not good for you,' a friend chides.

'I was wearing a respirator. I would have opened the hatches if it hadn't been raining so hard.'

As November winds down, I want to think that it is *Grace* who has taken my breath away, again. She did it when I first saw her tied to a seawall in the Florida Keys, the most beautiful girl at the high school dance. Two years have done nothing to dampen my infatuation. I often stop rowing when she first appears at anchor in the night.

But there is nothing romantic about this heaviness in

my chest. I pause at the top of the stairs, reaching for breath. I ought to call my doctor. A ten-day course of antibiotics would probably do the trick.

I intensify daily workouts instead; sessions that take on overtones of dread. *Push harder and cough the crap out.*

Reality comes to get me a few days after Christmas. During an afternoon stint on the Stairmaster, an ominous presence steps down on the centre of my chest. More than shortness of breath, this monster announces with dead-weight clarity that the workout stops. Now.

I lie down on the floor. In time the heaviness and pain beneath my sternum give way to cautious relief. I grimly concede that something is wrong. I talk to my doctor, Dr Jon Gans, that evening. We will meet at the hospital in the morning.

●●●●●

I REGISTER AT SPECTRUM HEALTH CENTER in Grand Rapids just after daybreak, and feel comfortable climbing on the treadmill for a cardiac stress test a short time afterwards. I have been running for twenty years, insulating myself from a family history littered with cardiac accidents. In spite of the morning's chill, I have worn running shoes and shorts.

'A jog in the park,' I tell the nurse, hoping that it is true.

Minutes into what is usually a light workout, I already have an unwelcome heaviness in my chest. Jon enters the room and signals for me to stop. I do not resist.

Standing down, I surprise myself by reaching out for steadiness. Jon glances at me directly, then looks away, shaking his head.

'I don't like what I see, John. I'd like to have one of our heart guys do an angiogram.'

He explains that they will anaesthetize me, open an artery in my groin, and run a catheter up into the arteries of my heart for an on-site inspection.

I hear the words, but I am a thousand miles away. Nothing in the room – not Jon, not the nurse, nor the proliferation of machines – is real to me. From a distance, I hear him referring to the procedure as 'the gold standard'.

Sensing my withdrawal, Jon steps closer, a hand on my forearm. 'We really *need* to do this.'

'When?' My voice sounds hollow.

'Now. It's not safe for you to leave the hospital until we know what we've got here.'

I leave the room again, an embodiment of denial. I want to tell him that this can't be true, remind him that I am a runner. I want to laugh, and to have him laugh back.

But there is distress in his averted eyes, for we are old friends. I can dismiss his words, but not his distress.

I am – at this moment – resident in an utterly changed life.

•••••

BARBARA NEEDS TO GET OUR GIRLS (eight-year-old Katie and four-year-old Erin) off to school before she can come to the hospital. Nineteen-year-old John Ryan will get himself off to college. I want Barbara here before we proceed. My concern about alarming her has me back in my body when she arrives. I share what little I know, our fingers intertwined.

Jon Gans joins us, making the case for immediate action. He patiently outlines the risk factors involved.

'This is the only way we're going to know how serious your heart problems are,' he reiterates, looking for an ally in Barbara. 'All we can do is speculate – without taking a firsthand look.'

Jon is not interested in speculation. He discourages any discussion about what they might discover. Reluctant references to blockage, angioplasty and open-heart surgery are more than enough. Barbara and I look at each other.

This is a moment we have tried to ward off for twenty years. All the exercise, the irregular attempts at moderation, all the *vegetables* – and still, here we are. Making a decision to proceed that is less a decision than a concession to inevitability.

'We have to do this to know, I guess.'

●●●●●

I DON'T WARM MUCH TO THE stainless steel wheelchair, and even less to the surgical gurney a corridor or two later. I try to be good-natured about the hapless attempts of the first technician to find a vein in my forearm. I don't like needles at all. Barbara strokes the back of my wrist as they usher in a phlebotomist for another go with the needles. Shortly after assuring me playfully that she never misses, she hits the target – on the second try.

'Surgery is going to be a piece of cake after this.'

The nurse who takes me down a short corridor has long, piano-player's fingers and tanned forearms. She wheels me around a corner and into the refrigerated brightness of surgery.

I feign lightheartedness with the blue-gowned technicians who hover over me in a flurry of preparation. They are thoroughly versed in gallows humour. How many times will they dance this dance today, with how many captive women and men? However extraordinary this seems to me, it is ordinary: another middle-aged man with a heart that doesn't work. Let's see why.

'This might feel funny,' she says, injecting a sedative into my arm.

• • • • •

I OPEN MY EYES TO BARBARA in the recovery room, her hand on my arm, a smile nobody deserves.

'How are you?'

'Goofy,' but it isn't a complaint.

I try to stay focused when Dr Besley shares his post-operative opinion with us. Grim and understated, he tells us that my Left Anterior Descending artery (LAD), one of three cardiac arteries, is almost entirely closed. The LAD is ghoulishly referred to as the 'widow maker' because it supplies blood to the left ventricle, the major pumping muscle of the heart. The blood-starved complaint of the muscle it supplies is the ache I feel in my chest. The good news is that I probably haven't had a full-blown heart attack yet.

Tomorrow they will perform an angioplasty, a less-invasive alternative to open-heart surgery. Dr Besley explains in detail how they will enter the incision in my groin and snake a catheter up into my heart, balloon open the blocked artery, and insert a metal stent to keep it open. He becomes very noncommittal when I raise the issue of the long sailing trip we have planned.

'We need to get this fixed first, then see what we've got to work with.'

In an ominous aside, he adds, 'Nobody would want to do open-heart surgery on itsy, bitsy arteries like yours.'

•••••

I HAVE DECIDED TO GET WELL. I am nuts about Barbara and our kids. I am surrounded by family and friends.

I have things to do. Barbara and I have a shared vision, a long-incubated dream of pulling anchor to sail the world. Katie and Erin will go with us. John Ryan will stay in Michigan to finish college, and join us when he can. We are scheduled to leave in eighteen months, to make our way through the Great Lakes to the Atlantic. There is no room in our timetable for a weakened heart or the insecurity that travels with it.

I have everything to live for.

I will get better.

It all seems possible as I burrow my feet into the beach sand at the base of the sea wall in Fort Lauderdale. The January sun warms my bare back, plies the soft angles of the bikinied group strewn out between me and the ocean. The balminess feels like safety, like good health.

It has been a week since my angioplasty, since I left the hospital, shaken. Only a week and I am back at the ocean's edge, already the beginnings of a tan. Invigorated by the sun and scenery, I can feel my animal energy again.

Out beyond the bathers the sun is sparkling on the Atlantic. Further out there's a sail on the horizon, a triangle of brightness riding a brisk Northerly through the building fetch of the contrary Gulf Stream current. Put upon, but making headway. Everything is possible.

Barry Johnson, a friend of several decades, caught a plane back to Michigan at noon. At Barbara's request, he had joined me for a recuperative stint in Florida. Being on my own now means the immediate danger has passed. My arteries are open again. The incision in my groin is healing. In spite of Dr Besley's diagnosis of 'severe coronary artery disease', things are looking up.

I cannot run yet, but I can begin long walks today. I brush off my feet and slip on my battered running shoes. I am soothed by their familiar feel, reassured by the memory of half-marathons Barbara and I have run, as well as a full marathon and a triathlon. Heart problems be damned: I am an athlete, with an athlete's resiliency. I'll be okay.

I start off slowly, feeling my way along. Four blocks and not a sliver of pain. I step up the pace for four more, still pain-free. Then I push into it. The sunblock-laced sweat stings my eyes. A drinking fountain bath and I am at it again, feeling the rhythm and the familiar tug in my calves and hamstrings. Over a mile now, smiling at passers-by with the joy of motion.

The pavement curls inland, away from the beach. I hit the corners hard – a medical miracle, the unstoppable bionic man. Sweat is running down my chest. My soaked running shorts feel like a victory over fear, over shortness of breath, over that heaviness in my chest.

Breath comes comfortably, even at a gathering pace in this afternoon heat. Long, deep breaths without the desperate gasp of the infirm. The western sun is in my eyes now, forcing my gaze down to the pavement in front of me. I don't care. Nothing can touch me. I am in motion, and I am okay.

I can see the long arch of a bridge ahead. Confident now, I am looking forward to the exertion this pace will demand on its steep incline. As I come up to a convenience store, I feel the first suggestion of pain in my chest. *Just a cramp*, I tell myself. *Push through it*. But instead of going away, it deepens, welling up under my sternum.

I slow my pace, a concession I make to Barbara and the kids. But the pain continues to build. The monster is standing on my chest again. My breathing is going haywire, my head full of carbonation. I am stopping now, bending over, holding my knees. My heart is aching. I ease myself down onto the ground.

As I lie in the grass next to the pavement, the world slowly returns to normal. In time, my head clears and my breathing becomes regular. The leaves above me shimmer in the breeze. The spasm in my chest eventually gives way, but not before shredding the hopes I have been hanging back up in my life. I am back at Ground Zero.

Hours later, showered and sprawling on a bed at my budget motel, I struggle to make sense of what happened out there. I did not imagine it, or bring it on with worry. Was it simply a case of too much exertion, too soon? Or is something still wrong?

I take refuge from questions I cannot answer in the sturdy knowledge that I come from a family of survivors: a flinty Irish mother who was supposed to perish from a heart defect as a child – dancing on the pavement in defiance of her doctor and still dancing up into her eighties;

and a hard-headed father, clinically dead of a heart attack on an emergency room table at fifty-one, but still ticking thirty years later. And I can't help but smile when I think of my older sister Diane, an authentic force-of-nature, fighting it out with both heart disease and cancer, still out there punching.

There is no room for heart failure in a life this full.

In spite of my resolve, uncertainty infects my remaining time in Florida. Every day erupts sunny and warm, an invitation out into the light. At night the tree frogs serenade outside my shadow-strewn room, an insistent anthem of eros and renewal. I lie awake on over-bleached sheets, listening in the darkness.

• • • • •

BACK IN GRAND RAPIDS THE FOLLOWING WEEK, I return to the routine of daily life: children to get up and off to school, clients to see, the children to pick up and ease into the evening. Beneath this thin film of normality, I am haunted by questions no one seems able to answer. My mind rarely strays far from the irregular ache in my chest.

Let go, I tell myself. *You're making yourself crazy.*

Everything is worse in the early hours of morning, when I am just rested enough to have trouble falling back to sleep. I try to focus on things that pull me into the future. I *need* a future. The trip we have planned – a long time out on open water – most often provides relief.

On other occasions I take refuge in the memory of our first improbable journey to the sea. Uncertainty recedes when I step back into the ever-available past. On one particularly tormented early morning, I escape altogether and revisit the beginning . . .

●●●●●

IT IS THE SPRING OF 1984. Barbara and I are wringing our hands over happy-hour libations, whining playfully about how hard we are working. We both love our jobs, Barbara as an attorney and I as a clinical psychologist. We are, however, having trouble reviving our flagging energies during the week-long holidays we compress between months of super-charged effort.

'What we need are longer holidays.'

'About a year.'

'Let's take a year then.' My mouth is ahead of my brain.

Barbara looks, but doesn't reply.

'Let's work hard for five years, then take a year off,' I continue. 'A sabbatical.'

'Who'll pay for it?'

'We will. We have five years to save.'

Barbara knows a good thing when she hears it. 'What do we do with the year?'

'Let's get a motorcycle and tour Europe and Africa.' *Where did that come from?*

'Are you ready to put John Ryan – he'll be thirteen then – behind the handlebars?'

I pull up short.

'How about going sailing?' I have seen the adverts: the steaming cup of coffee at sunrise, the first mate's satisfied smile, the allure of the horizon.

'Sure.' Barbara is fully engaged now, slowing only to

point out, 'We don't know how to sail. And we don't have a boat . . . or a bank account.'

'We have five years to get ready,' I quip hormonally.

Don't put it out in front of Barbara if you're not ready to deliver. She takes her adventures seriously. She does not flinch when I bring up 'our cruise' in subsequent weeks. As the winter groans on, the idea morphs into a shared dream, and later still, a plan.

First we have to get a boat. This will not be easy. We have no money. We also know nothing about boats.

We do what we can, and begin saving immediately. A tight budget pays quick dividends. 'Do we want it?' gives way to 'Do we need it?' in our discussions. We discover – even as we begin to accumulate some savings – that we live better when we purchase less. We solve problems rather than trying to buy our way out of them, and we talk more.

As austere as it might sound, we don't miss what we don't need. A less expensive house and two 10-year-old cars are plenty. With less 'stuff,' our relationship becomes more important. Saving becomes a game, equal parts discipline and dream. Working on it together deepens our connection.

Because we know nothing about boats, we read everything we can. Barbara specializes in 'how to' books while I read adventure stories. She consequently learns the name of boat parts and equipment, vocabulary that still eludes me. Together we prowl the docks of West Michigan, grilling any sailor who ventures eye contact. We mostly ask primitive questions. Sailors, who almost universally love to talk about their boats, warm to our interest, and we take their willingness to its limits.

With more enthusiasm than money, we drive a shrinking number of boat dealers to agitation with miserly bids on better and better boats. In time, the brokers pretend not to see us when we enter a boatyard. It's not a sentiment I enjoy inspiring, but it's one I can live with. *Go with what you've got:* in our case big dreams, a tight budget, and growing clarity about what we want in a boat.

Almost two years into the process, we get a 10pm call from a broker we have long tormented. Armed with flashlights, Barbara, John Ryan and I take a midnight tour of a two-year-old C&C-designed Canadian sloop. She is more racer than cruiser, but she is strong and immaculately maintained. She will go on the market in the morning. Our offer of less than is owed on the boat elicits an exasperated moan.

'Damnit, John. He'll be so offended by this bid, he won't even talk with you.'

When I later try to dampen John Ryan's enthusiasm in the parking lot, he will have none of it.

'Dad, this boat is our destiny.'

At 10am the following morning, my secretary buzzes me during a session.

'I'm sorry, John. He says it is urgent.'

'Are you sitting down?' Bruce opens. Caught off guard, I say nothing.

'What are you going to name your boat?'

At our bank, two weeks later, a blindly optimistic mortgage banker takes a deep breath, looks the other way, and approves our loan. Barbara and I glance at each other, barely able to suppress our laughter. We decide to call our boat what she is: *Outrageous.*

For three short Michigan summers we learn to sail the best way we know: we sail. From April's last snowfall to November's first, we sail. We rarely sail by the book. Our frequent mistakes elicit smiles in some quarters and open derision in others. We sail in good weather and – more importantly – in bad. When the other boats come in against the backdrop of foreboding skies, we go out.

'Got to find out what to do when it really gets rough out here.'

Our mistakes are legendary and our learning curve is steep, but with experience comes the growing sense that we can do it.

We don't anticipate a surprise pregnancy, however, a scant sixteen months before we plan to leave. Our parents and friends see it as a welcome excuse for us to come to our senses, and in spite of our public posturing, there is more than a little hesitation in our private discussions.

'It's not fair to saddle a child with the legacy of an abandoned dream,' I argue. Barbara agrees. So within weeks of her birth, we take Katie on her first Northern Michigan sailing holiday. It is deep into the autumn, but we simply must test our limits. Katie, until recently afloat on a sea of her own, adapts easily, in spite of the snow flurries that blow in for several of our seven days. We heave a sigh of relief, then renew our increasingly frantic preparations for life at sea.

'Let's go for it,' is all that Barbara has to say.

Eight months later, in the summer of 1989, Barry Johnson, Dan Hendrickson and I sail *Outrageous* across the Atlantic. Barbara, John Ryan and baby Kate join me for a summer and autumn cruise in the Mediterranean.

After we get hammered by a storm off the Atlantic coast of North Africa, I sail *Outrageous* singlehandedly back across to the Caribbean. Barbara and the kids join me there for a winter and spring of island-hopping, and we head back to Michigan in the summer of 1990.

'Not long enough' is an oft-repeated chorus as we point the bow for home. But we have promised to have John Ryan back to start high school. We begin planning the next trip – 'a longer one' – as we motor up the Hudson and through the Erie Canal to the Great Lakes.

•••••

I FUMBLE FOR THE ALARM CLOCK that yanks me out of my reverie. I am stranded on this still-dark shore, in the first faint outlines of this approaching day. The limits of memory, and the ease of dismay.

We did it once, I remind myself, rolling over to where Barbara is sleeping.

Maybe we can do it again.

•••••

JANUARY GIVES WAY TO FEBRUARY, the darkest month in West Michigan. Cloudy days pile up, one upon another, stealing whole weeks of sunshine. In what is always a challenging month for the melancholy Irishman in me, I set new standards for muddling through. The painful episodes continue – not as dramatic as the one in Florida – despite a Thallium stress test which yields only a 'very soft finding' of heart malfunction with exercise.

What the medical technology can't capture is the ache that joins me for my daily walk and in the evening when we are making love. I stubbornly refuse to curtail either, making my way through the pain at a slower pace, a nitro-glycerin under my tongue. I wait for the medicinal magic to kick in. I should get relief in minutes.

If I let pain run my life, I'll end up a cripple.

Despite my resolve to make no unnecessary conces-sions, each new incident erodes my sense of well-being and feeds a lingering and growing doubt that something is not right.

I want to believe the pain is hypochondriacal, a phys-ical manifestation of my thoroughly shaken confidence. If this is only in my mind, if I am somehow causing these episodes with my preoccupation and insecurity, they will go away with time. I will not alter my life in their honour, or install them as even minor gods at the centre of my daily existence.

Barbara travels these back roads with me, as do several longstanding friends. I try to be open and honest with them, fighting my way through my own editing process to what is really going on. My disdain for whining makes it confusing. Where does forthrightness end and victim-hood begin? I don't deal with befuddlement gracefully, cutting myself little slack when I feel that openness has deteriorated into complaint.

For years I have been telling clients and students how woundedness can entrap us in self-absorption, tether and constrict, and turn us by way of smaller and smaller circles in on ourselves. I now struggle day and night to avoid being swallowed up in my own spiral of vulnerability and insecurity. I resist the billowing fear that life as I have known it is being taken away, but wherever I go, there is something else there with me: a portentous shadow that will neither confront me face-to-face nor leave me alone, even for an hour. *Something is still wrong*.

•••••

I ANCHOR MY LIFE TO BARBARA and the children, and – to a lesser extent – to my work.

The kids provide almost instant relief from the claustrophobia of self-absorption. They invite me directly into their lives, at various stages of work in progress. The little girls have attention spans too short to be preoccupied with the saga of my aching heart, and in any case we try to shield them as much as possible.

Erin's life is infused with the magic of someone unprotected by guile. Her running commentary on how the world works keeps all of us entertained. She holds court from under a mop of shiny brown hair, fringe half-concealing the gleam in her eyes. Nothing escapes her scrutiny, or the uncensored analysis she is eager to share. She greets Barbara's attempt to camouflage the strain with 'What's wrong? It's going to be okay, Mommy,' complete with a pat on the hand or arm. Erin feels what she does not know, and crawls with increasing regularity into daddy's lap for long and soulful hugs. Sometimes she falls asleep there, drawing me along.

Katie, with her sea-blue eyes and a bundle of freckles, lives comfortably in the physical world. Her perpetually skinned elbows and knees are badges of honour. The only thing better than watching a sporting event is taking out the football and heading for an open field. Life is a game of tag, a tangle of blonde hair trailing out behind. Any event she can rope dad into – a long bike ride, wrestling on the rug – is already a win. A win for dad also.

John Ryan is my son from a marriage that turned out to be an enduring friendship instead. His mother, Chris, has co-parented him with Barbara and me. His late-adolescent abandon regularly leaves all of us breathless. For several years my North is his South, the hard work of declaring independence. Whenever I am about to emancipate his head from the rest of him, he reminds me that 'Nobody said this was going to be easy, Dad,' and melts my resolve in a glance. I am alternately terrified and enthralled by the stage show that is his life, and willing captive of his exploits.

Anything I say about Barbara will sound like an exaggeration. I am crazy about her, a state I now call 'normal'. On that dense and unearned footing we have built a relationship I am incapable of doubting, even in my darkest moments. We are going through this together, wherever it leads.

Work helps. I like my job as a clinical psychologist, even on difficult days. I have my own private practice, and I meet on an hourly basis with people I care for, clients but also friends. We attempt transparency during our time together, trying to make sense of the riddles that are life. I get to watch people grow. That I get paid for this continues to amaze me.

I have doting parents, a sister and brother that I admire and love, and a cadre of close friends, several dating back to childhood. I have a lot to be grateful for, and precious little to complain about. In spite of all these advantages, I long for a lost sense of security. I pad my days with what I hope is a healthy routine: a period of quiet time, whatever exercise my pain will allow, and a handful of pills, morning and night. I want to do better than languish, waiting for the other shoe to drop.

Regular blood tests have everyone smiling. 'Great lipid profile,' they pronounce. No one has an explanation for the irregular ache in my chest, and I am reluctant to mention it, as if I am doing something wrong.

• • • • •

WE STRAGGLE INTO MARCH, the first sustained thaws. But there is no thaw in my chest, where a nagging pain returns with any physical exertion. I am learning to live with it, resorting to nitroglycerin only when the pain reaches ominous proportions. It is Wagnerian background music for a life that largely works.

When pain yanks me out of a dead sleep at 1am in early March, I am startled. *This is different.* I fumble for my nitro, rousing Barbara in the process.

'Sorry to wake you. I'm in trouble.'

The monster is standing on my chest. Both feet, bigger and heavier than before, pain running up into my neck. I open and close the fingers of my left hand, waiting for the nitro to kick in. Nothing. I slip a second nitro under my tongue. I have long forgiven its acrid taste, for it has become my friend. It will help me. In a few more seconds I will get relief.

Barbara is wide awake, trying to be calm when I refuse the suggested call to an Emergency Unit. 'It will freak out the kids. Let's wait and see if this works.'

It does help, a bit, in minutes that register like hours. The third nitro – 'I know I'm not supposed to' – gradually takes the pain down a notch. It does not go away. It gives no sign of going away.

I need to get to the hospital. John Ryan is not home, so a friend will stay with our sleeping girls. I cautiously slip on sandals, a sweatshirt and sweatpants, anticipating disrobing if an emergency room visit metastasizes into full-blown hospitalization. Barbara and I ease gingerly down the stairs and out into the yard. *Will walking on tiptoes fool my heart?*

Barbara draws the line when I move to the driver's side door. She drives to the hospital slowly, as if it will soothe the ache. Had *slow* been a more natural pace, perhaps we wouldn't be going to the hospital at all. I don't tell her about my dread of going there, the resistance of the truly terrified. Perhaps I would relax if it were not for the needles, and the multiple pokes required to find a vein. One for this test, a second for that, a third for the intravenous line.

The hospital dance is rejoined: the crisis-calloused triage nurse, the blurry-eyed third shifters, the swoosh of the privacy curtain, the nitroglycerin paste, the needles, the exhausted resident doctor, the hushed urgency of phone calls. The on-call cardiologist announces the inevitable: 'We're going to have to admit you, John.'

Barbara and I glance at each other: no reference to 'adventure' tonight. We are stretched a little too thin for that.

After a long ride through strangely deserted corridors, I am ushered from the elevator to an observation room.

By dawn I am exhausted by the non-stop visits from solicitous nurses. I have convinced Barbara to return home to
get some sleep in anticipation of another long day. The
kids will be awake soon. They will need explanation and
support, and more strenuous pre-school promptings than
usual.

'I'm not going anywhere but to sleep,' I assure her.

• • • • •

INTO MY DELIRIOUS EXHAUSTION sweeps Dr Rick McNamara.
An associate of Dr Besley, who is on holiday, Rick is Chief
Cardiologist of the hospital. We first met eight years ago,
before his curly hair went white. His somewhat haggard face
belies his native wattage, the playful gleam in his eyes. I like
him immediately. Since I often work with doctors, we quickly
shift to a comfortable first-name basis.

Preliminaries aside, Rick tells me what I already know:
'We'll have to go back in to find out what's going on.'

It is a familiar routine by now, for which I have a
fear I call contempt. I am strangely comforted that he
will be doing the cutting, a trust that he has not yet
earned.

'If it's all blocked up – and you think you can fix it
with your balloons and stents – you don't have to wake
me up for approval. Just do what you need to do while
you're in there.'

'Right,' he nods, a little taken back by my premature
confidence. 'See you in a few minutes.' He will work me
in before his first scheduled surgery. He is gone.

The instant rapport I have with him dilutes some of
the dread I have about another trip to surgery. I wish

Barbara was here, but she might not arrive until I am in surgery. She is where we need her to be. There are no real decisions to make, and she'll be here by the time I get out.

•••••

WHEN I OPEN MY EYES SEVERAL HOURS LATER in the recovery room, Barbara is sitting on the edge of the bed, a hand over my heart. At close range, she listens with her body.

'Steady as she goes, big boy.'

We just get into my questions about the kids when Rick flies through the privacy curtains. *Is this guy drinking too much coffee?* He meets Barbara like a long-lost friend. Were he less charming, or I so inclined, I could resent the instant intimacy we have. Barbara likes him as quickly as I.

'We know what's been causing your pain, John. Your LAD artery was almost entirely closed. Again.' Rick lets it register.

'In spite of this attack, you apparently have not suffered significant heart damage.'

'That's good,' I monitor the expression on Barbara's face.

'So what did you do?' I prod.

'We've got that artery pretty well opened up. Let's hope it stays that way.'

'Hope?'

'The numbers aren't so good for someone whose arteries have closed back up as quickly as yours.'

'They might close up again?'

'They might.'

I'm too foggy to pursue this further. I glance at Barbara, trying to camouflage my disappointment.

'Let's talk about this some more when you're feeling better,' Rick counsels, 'more wide awake.'

Whatever energy I had is expended. Everything gets very fuzzy again.

• • • • •

I AWAKE TO THE WELCOME STERILITY OF MY ROOM. I am alone. The now familiar sandbags are piled on my groin, pinning me in place. I am not allowed to move until the bleeding stops. Blood-thinning medicine has made me porous; a shaving cut can take an hour to quench. The accumulating incisions in the large artery in my groin take longer and longer to close.

My eyes adjust to the sunlight outside. A window so clear it has disappeared. For a few moments I am free in the fields beyond. Some women from the local college are limbering up, their arms and legs thrust out at odd angles in this first, early hint of warmth. A track team, perhaps. A spring invitation, a mockery of my sorry state.

A good time to heal, I tell myself. The sun calls out the vitality dormant in all of us. These incisions will close over. My arteries are open. My heart can breathe again. Perhaps the pain will be gone altogether. Perhaps this nightmare is over.

The door opens a crack and Barbara smiles in. She has been at the office making phone calls. Several days of our clients' appointments have been pushed back. We need some breathing room.

As an attorney with a private practice of her own, Barbara can tailor her schedule to the needs of our children. I have similar control over my schedule, ensuring us an enviable degree of flexibility. We need the flexibility now, but our control still seems lame in the face of the rampage in which we are adrift.

Barbara and Rick have scheduled a follow-up consultation, which begins shortly. He is done with surgery for the day, and relaxation ebbs into the taut weariness around his eyes and mouth. He is available, if not eager, to deal with hard questions.

He patiently explains about re-stenosis, a largely mysterious aberration in the arterial healing process where injured vessels gradually close up. Complete closure of any one of my narrowed coronary arteries will result in a major heart attack, and the oxygen-starved death of those portions of the heart's muscle nourished by the artery. Survival depends on the severity of damage. Because a dead heart muscle never regenerates, you live or die with what's left over.

Rick is very direct in his assessment of my re-stenosis: 'What I fixed may not stay fixed.'

'What happens if it closes up again?'

'We can do another angioplasty, if the vessels will tolerate it.' After a pause, he adds . . . 'Or we may have to look at open-heart surgery, at bypassing the most damaged areas of the arteries.'

In the back of my head there is a muffled explosion, the activated discomfort with Dr Besley's first postoperative analysis: *'Nobody would want to do open-heart surgery on itsy, bitsy arteries like yours.'*

'Dr Besley said those arteries of mine are pretty small.'

'They're awfully small, John. That's genetic, nothing you or we can do anything about. I'll run your x-rays and scans by our open heart guys. We'll plan for every contingency.'

I break a long, awkward pause. 'Now, what about the good news?'

Our smiles fade as he reaches a little too far for an answer. 'There are some very faint collaterals in there; your heart's attempt to bypass that clogged LAD. They may be the reason you didn't have a major heart attack. We can hope you're one of those people who spontaneously grow them, a kind of genetic payback for those miniature cardiac arteries of yours. While they can never replace normal arterial flow, they can help.'

'Anything I can do to help them grow?'

'A lot of it is hereditary, John. But Barbara tells me you have those lucky Irish genes. That could help.'

Grins all around. Grins on an afternoon with little to grin about, except maybe the first stirrings of spring, the pretty young runners leaning into the corners of the oval track outside.

• • • • •

THEY LET ME GO HOME THE NEXT DAY. During the ensuing weeks, Michigan extricates itself from the harshness of winter. Buds arrive early, a nod in the direction of summer's warmth. On sunny days I meet clients for sessions over outdoor tables at a local coffee shop. Awash in the depressive lag that lingers after every surgery, I am hungry for the uplift of sunlight.

Barbara and I work to normalize what can be made normal, to put a floor under ourselves and the kids. The girls are young enough to take their cues from us, and quickly pop back to the surface. John Ryan, familiar with my disdain for victimhood, alternates between playful derision of my deterioration and stern lectures about 'being smart' when he thinks I overdo it.

I am taken aback by the concern showed me by my family, clients and friends. *So this is what community is about?* An incorrigible show-off, I am awkward in the face of their unsolicited attention. I try to relax down into it, without analysis. Like the scant arteries in my heart, it is just what it is.

Barbara and I pry time away for ourselves, frequently returning to our planned sailing trip. I cling to it with grim tenacity, my lifeline in the riptide of my fleeing health. I drag three of my most dexterous friends into the scheme, huddling with them one Saturday in April to brainstorm the transformation of our second boat, *Grace*, into a family-friendly cruiser.

Grace is the offspring of our first, sixteen-month cruise on *Outrageous*. By the time we returned to the Great Lakes with John Ryan and Katie in 1990, Barbara and I had decided to go 'out there' again, 'only longer next time'. We regularly discussed the feasibility of a heavier, ocean-going cruiser for that next trip, and Erin's arrival on the scene two years later cemented our commitment to a larger, sturdier boat.

Grace sailed into our lives two years after Erin. She is a 50ft, Bill Tripp-designed, cutter-rigged ocean cruiser. Her 67ft mast and twin foresail configuration can handle a full complement of sails. She has an uncluttered teak deck, a small doghouse cabin and a narrow beam, giving her a sleek, classic profile. She is strong and fast and easy on the eyes. She does however need extensive renovation below deck, which is why I am rallying the troops.

Dan Hendrickson, a friend for almost twenty years, is an accomplished sailor. We sold him *Outrageous* when we purchased *Grace*. Dan also has a long-term interest in carpentry, with skills to match. He brings a sense of playfulness to even the most serious endeavours: 'Building things keeps me from committing suicide in Michigan winters,' he quips.

I've known David Doyle, a spindly leprechaun from the neighbourhood, since we went to school together. We intersect at places both serious and absurd: from progressive politics to the obtuse intricacies of Notre Dame football. David's sense of humour ripens as his thinning hair goes white. He claims to welcome immersion in electrical work and plumbing, 'where you can see the results right away, hold them in your hands.'

Barry Johnson and I met as naïve appointees to a do-nothing municipal committee on race relations in the early seventies. Barry's angular Nordic features have weathered over time, but not his good-natured passion for 'big, hairy projects' and University of Michigan football. Like Dan and David, he likes to get his hands dirty.

The four of us swap ideas about how to build sea berths for Katie and Erin. I want them to have separate rooms: small places they can call their own with doors they can slam when adolescence takes them over.

The process of redesigning *Grace* is thoroughly engrossing, and welcome relief from the powerlessness I feel to fix my heart. How to fashion safe and comfortable bedrooms without undermining the boat's structural integrity, plumbing or electronics? How to do this within the fluid curvature of the hull?

Possessing marginal to non-existent skills as a carpenter, plumber, or electrician, I will need to borrow egregiously from the abilities of my friends. I will learn as I go. It is a now familiar ritual for them, keeping my head above water while I embark on that next great scheme. After the initial head-scratching and scepticism, they will show up for even the dirtiest of the dirty work, gathering a new set of stories, well-freighted with derision, with which to abuse me when I get too far out of line.

Remember that time . . .

David leaves in the late afternoon, Dan and Barry an hour later. I linger on *Grace* after they go, drawing energy from the changes we have planned. I pull myself up the companionway and lie down on a cockpit settee. The early spring sun is almost warm. I unzip the top of my jacket and exhale. Not a whiff of discomfort in my chest, in spite of the underlying chill. *This is not the first time they have bailed me out.* Another long breath – deeper this time – and I let go, riding the breath down into the reassurance of memory, the first trans-Atlantic crossing . . .

• • • • •

IT IS JUNE 1989, a humid midday in Hampton, Virginia. Barry, Dan and I are soaking wet, the exertion over last provisions running down our shoulders and chests, dripping onto the cabin sole. We are jamming bulky packages of Huggies into the aft cabin of *Outrageous*. Katie – who, with her mother and John Ryan, will replace Dan and Barry in Gibraltar – is months away from being toilet trained.

'Get the camera,' Barry laughs.

Within hours we are nearing the mouth of the Chesapeake, hell-bent for the Atlantic. We are schedule-driven
and dumb, unaware of what awaits us. None of us has
sailed in the ocean before. We have a geography class
knowledge of the Gulf Stream and Hatteras. We have not
even listened to a weather forecast.

'We sailed across Lake Michigan ...'

'Seen one, seen them all.'

I admit to concern about the black clouds piling up in
the North, rolling down towards us.

'Come on, John ...'

We are already behind schedule, we remind each other,
casualties of a damaged forestay. It is the brashness of the
uninitiated.

The storm grinds in before dark, just as we are entering
the Gulf Stream. It is a saltwater nightmare, waves arching
over the boat. The three-dimensional delirium of pitch, roll
and yaw turns our chemistry against us. We take turns at
the wheel, our eyes wide at the harsh angles of the waves.
In my ignorance I wish for dawn, to be able to see what
we have entered.

The edge goes out of it by the following afternoon, and
the sun breaks through. We are feeling better until Dan
sticks his head up the companionway.

'Something's wrong. Our electronics are gone.'

A hurried inspection confirms our worst fears. A small
river of saltwater has trickled down from an unseen break
along the toerail, soaking the circuit panel that is the heart
of our electrical system. The adjacent single sideband radio
and satnav have shared the deadly bath, water dripping
from the bottom of their cases.

'We can get along without the rest,' I am trying to be calm, 'but we won't know where we are without the sat nav.'

The thought of going back is intolerable. It has taken too long to break free. The clock is running on Dan and Barry's holiday schedules. Jobs only wait so long.

'We do have a plastic sextant somewhere, and a book on how to use it. You've got that fancy calculator, Dan.'

'Damn, John . . .'

'And we know about where we are, our latitude. At worst we can head due East.'

'If the fishermen are white when we get to the other side, we'll turn right . . .'

'And if they're black, we'll turn left . . .'

'Then follow the big boats in . . .'

We straggle into Gibraltar six weeks later, a signal victory of tenacity and imagination over inexperience. *Outrageous* has paid a high price – a broken forestay and a shredded mainsail – and I am clearly the weakest link, having struggled with a chronic, low-grade seasickness.

I have swallowed the ocean whole. Or has she swallowed me?

• • • • •

BACK IN THE COCKPIT OF *GRACE*, a first involuntary shudder calls me out of reminiscence. The beginning of a chill in this ebbing afternoon, with a now plunging sun. And later, on the overheated ride back home, a renewed sense of slope-shouldered survivability.

• • • • •

THE BOATYARD AT CROSSWINDS MARINA in Whitehall begins to fill on the weekends. Tarps are stripped away, the toxic odour of anti-fouling paint. The whining sanders accompany the good-natured complaints about waxing hulls. Endless bags of sails are hauled out, bottles of bleach to fight back insistent mould. Engines and water systems are flushed, stress points greased, and shrouds adjusted. Belts, lights and worn impellers are replaced.

'Isn't yachting glamorous?' I joke with anyone whose shoulders sag even a little. There is no place any of us would rather be.

Within this hothouse of activity, vague rumours spread about my health. I regularly have to stop midstream to field well-intentioned questions. I listen to war stories from other cardiac veterans, survivors with enough water beneath them to talk comfortably about their misadventures. I appreciate their concern, but I am still in free-fall. I have no victories to announce, only uncertainty and resolve.

'So I guess this puts a crimp in your plans to leave next year?'

My thin confidence does little to convince. Lots of head-shaking, and occasional averted eyes. I'm sure some think we're damn fools for even considering going out there, but whatever their reservations, they wish me well. I cannot blame them for having the same doubts that regularly visit me.

Over a late-night dinner together, I re-examine Barbara's resolve.

'They know *I'm* crazy, but *you* are going to take a lot of heat as the time winds down . . . *if* we're still set on going.'

'I don't care about heat. I do care about your health, about you being well enough that we feel comfortable going.'

When I say nothing, Barbara adds an emphatic 'I *want* to go. We're going to get through this. I'm *planning* on our going.'

It's all I need and more.

•••••

'OH, GOD, NOT AGAIN!'

I am jolted awake at 3am in the first week of June, blurting anger that is really fear. The pain that has seeped back in small doses during recent workouts is on top of me, worse than ever, squeezing the breath out of me.

'What's wrong?' Barbara wakes with a spasm.

I cannot answer her.

'Are you okay?' She is up on her elbow beside me now, clearly alarmed.

'No, I'm not.'

She grabs the bottle of nitro we keep on a bookshelf above our heads. I open my mouth. She slips a tablet under my tongue. I hold it there, press my tongue down, wait for the spreading bitterness that precedes relief.

There is no relief until the third nitro has dissolved, then only a little.

The brief debate about an Emergency Unit is renewed, with similar results. We will dress and drive to the hospital. John Ryan will stay with his sleeping sisters.

The pain is easing somewhat. The dread is only beginning again, more bitter than nitro.

There is no discussion of who will drive this time. Barbara slips into the driver's seat and steers cautiously into the almost balmy June night. It is mild enough to roll the windows down. I drift away from the ache in my chest, into the spell the street lights fashion in the overhanging trees. My brain goes numb, leaves me dazed and sentient.

I do not resist the despised wheelchair at the emergency room, or the perfunctory questions at the triage desk. I am under the bright lights now, clothes being taken off, the gown that isn't, the needles and the gentle interrogation. Haven't we done all of this before? They mainline the heparin and tape on the nitro patch while they wait for the first set of blood tests to be analyzed. At some point they respectfully announce what we already know: I am not going home.

Their provisional diagnosis: 'Crescendo angina.' This puppy isn't getting enough blood to his heart.

Let's not go the next step, that steep descent into full cardiac seizure.

All I can do is to stay calm, cheer up Barbara and a string of sleepy doctors, and relax as deeply as possible. Barbara sits by my bed, trying to swallow her own private ache. Is there any good news here?

Later I am moved to an observation room upstairs. They monitor everything that can be monitored, interrupting any sleep I can find. I ask Barbara to go home. She won't. She leaves for a while to phone John Ryan. They plot strategies for dealing with the girls.

Here we go again.

• • • • •

RICK MCNAMARA ARRIVES BEFORE 7AM, more sombre than usual. *I only have to deal with this occasionally. He does it every day.*

'You don't look so good, Doctor. Who's the patient here?'

He smirks, but says nothing. We both know this isn't good.

'I hope you feel better than you look,' I re-load. 'I don't want a drowsy surgeon poking around in my heart.'

Rick grins weakly, then shakes his head and looks down. *No, this isn't good.*

'We have to go back in there, take another look, John.' He glances at Barbara and adds, 'There's nothing in the labs to indicate major heart damage yet, but something's blocking the blood flow.'

None of us has anything to say for several moments.

Rick breaks our silence. 'Try to get some rest – both of you. I'll work you into the schedule first thing. We've got another long day.'

• • • • •

BY AFTERNOON I AM BACK in my now-familiar room. I slip in and out of consciousness. Any lapse into deep sleep will assuredly be interrupted by a solicitous nurse, a reassuring 'you're doing fine.' Sometimes a hand on my wrist, which I carry with me when I close my eyes.

Barbara has caught a couple of hours' sleep and gone off to work. She is probably picking up the girls now, enduring their barrage of questions, soothing their fears.

At my insistence, John Ryan will bring them in tonight. They need to see for themselves that dad is okay, and get reacquainted with the hospital. There will be no quick exit this time.

In response to my questions, a nurse checks with the front desk. Rick will meet with Barbara and me at 5pm. He begged out of our usual postoperative session, telling us he wanted to talk when I was 'fully awake'. Fully awake is not possible on the scraps of sleep I get.

The women's track team is not out practising today. It might have helped. Instead, there's a rag-tag clot of teenage boys, their exercise regime supervised tentatively by a middle-aged man. At one point, several of his underlings fly off into a hard knot, tumbling and pounding away at each other. The supervisor intervenes only when real damage is imminent. Maybe years of experience have imparted some special understanding, an economy of motion. Maybe he's too wise to attempt control, or too worn out.

I grew up in a working class neighbourhood, the runt of the litter. I was the smallest boy at every age, until propelled past the others by a late growth spurt at sixteen.

The template was in place by then. You stayed on your feet in every fight. If you didn't break them with a maniacal early flurry – 'this kid is crazy' – you refused to stay down when pure poundage took over. You dragged yourself to your feet over and over until their energy or their will waned. 'This kid *is* crazy!' On my personalized scorecard, I won the fight if they walked away. They would eventually walk away if I kept getting up.

I mostly avoided fights when I could, throwing my last

punch at twenty-one when I stepped awkwardly between a man and the young woman he was harassing.

The body remembers its trips to the arena long after open warfare ceases. I have an immediate and primitive alliance with every underdog, reasonable or not, and an all-too-available rage toward any bully, which strains at the leash of my avowed nonviolence. The adrenaline thrust sets my heart racing, muscles all atwitch.

My history ushers me instinctively into the civil rights and anti-war movements that sweep over college campuses in the sixties. The assassinations of Dr King and Robert Kennedy only harden my resolve to make a difference. After finishing a doctorate in clinical psychology at Saint Louis University, I return to Grand Rapids where I am elected to eight years of thinly veiled combat in the Michigan House of Representatives and the Michigan Senate. The Legislature is no place for the impatient. Eighty-hour work weeks and chronic distress at the glacial pace of change gather in my belly like a clot. Carl Levin dispatches me in the Democratic primary during a premature run for the US Senate, probably saving my life. I am reassured that the best-equipped person sometimes wins.

A Republican reapportionment three years later completes the job. I return to the welcome decompression of my profession. Forty-hour work weeks with people I admire and results I can hold in my hands. Time for a personal life, for family and friends. Collaboration rather than competition. Life outside the combat zone.

Those frenetic years have taken their toll, however. No amount of exercise can erase what the body learns early, the enduring lessons of hard places. Some evenings I must turn off the national news and take the kids and our dog for a walk. The time bomb in my chest ticks on, even in more peaceful environs.

I open my eyes. Another battle has erupted in the field outside. I would trade places with the tired supervisor. However futile it might be, I would try to intervene.

•••••

RICK BLOWS INTO THE ROOM LIKE A STORMFRONT, his face sagging, too weary for subtlety.

'Bad news, John. The LAD is completely closed. Your right cardiac artery is also in trouble, very blocked up.' *Two out of three, more than a squall.*

I want to ask for the 'good news', looking for relief. Barbara and I are silent.

'We are beyond the point where another angioplasty is feasible,' Rick continues. The boat is lurching wildly now, unable to recover from one breaking wave before the next arrives . . . 'And our surgeons aren't that keen on trying to bypass arteries this small, this damaged.' We are sideways when the big one hits, rolling the boat with icy efficiency.

'I've talked to several of the best guys around the country – they want to see our x-rays and scans, of course – and I'm thinking that Johnson's group at St Francis in Milwaukee might be our best bet.' Somehow the boat rights itself, sails rising ghost-like and trembling, shaking off the foam.

'Best bet for what?' Barbara asks, filling the gap Rick has left for me.

'That's ultimately their call. They are the country's miracle workers with endarterectomies. I think that's our best hope.' *Best hope?*

Rick patiently explains the intricacies of an endarter-ectomy: slicing arteries lengthwise, stripping them of blockage, and splicing them back together, with patches harvested from other blood vessels.

'These guys are *something*,' Rick is as upbeat as he is able. 'They take on cases other surgeons won't.' *Other surgeons won't? This is the good news?*

Rick reads my face. 'The good news is that your heart muscles are still largely intact. You have sustained some damage, but you've got a hell of a strong heart.' *That's it?*

'. . . And you're a fighter,' he adds without a hint of question. A lifeline.

I grab it. 'With a hot girlfriend . . .' My voice breaks somewhat as I look at Barbara, 'and a long cruise to take.'

Barbara's resolve melts momentarily, her eyes moist even as she tries to smile back.

• • • • •

JOHN RYAN AND HIS SISTERS ARRIVE soon after Rick leaves. The girls head for the bed in a flurry, pulling up with alarm when they see the tubes running down into my arms.

'It's okay. It's how they give me medicine.' I try to reassure them with a smile and open arms.

'You can hug Daddy. Just be careful not to touch those sandbags,' Barbara adds.

The girls stand at the edge of the bed, full of questions and hesitation. John Ryan wades in, leaning over to hug me gingerly.

'Hey, Pops, I stopped by earlier. You were asleep and looked terrible, so I didn't wake you up. You *still* look terrible,' he jabs, a wide grin on his face.

'I love you too, hotshot,' the best I can come up with.

The girls follow John's lead, making their way up onto the bed with uncharacteristic restraint. It is unwitting testimony to my sorry state. For the first time in their lives, their father seems physically vulnerable. They don't like it, tears welling up in their eyes. Neither do I.

The girls make a strong recovery until it's time to go home. John Ryan will get them ready for bed.

'You can stay up until I get home,' Barbara assures. 'Soon.'

When they are gone, Barbara sits by the bed in silence. We are both running on empty.

'Let's get some sleep and see how it looks tomorrow.'

We hold on desperately when we hug, needles be damned.

As she goes out the door, I call to her. She sticks her head back in.

'We're going to get through this just fine,' I am trying to rally. 'Piece of cake.'

It backfires.

She pulls her head back from the doorway just as her smile dissolves to tears. My stomach convulses when I hear her break down in the corridor.

●●●●●

RICK GETS ME A GREEN LIGHT for surgery in Milwaukee. 'Our best hope, John.'

Later that night, he dictates his case summary: The LAD is a 'severely, diffusely diseased vessel . . . very minute vessel. On prior angiograms this was a much larger vessel.'

He describes the previously intact right cardiac artery as 'calcified, with significant diffuse disease,' lesions of 70% and 75% throughout.

That's two out of three.

He concludes: 'Very difficult situation here . . . patient understands that there may be long-term poor success, at best low patency, despite any intervention.'

• • • • •

TRANSPORT DAY FINALLY ARRIVES, not without its challenges. Unclip this and fasten that; trade the big monitors for mobile ones; load up extra hours of intravenous drips; take some of the electrodes off.

The first ambulance team arrives. Their fumbling belies what I hope is competence. Two of them stand around aimlessly, watching a third do all of the work. Perhaps they are trainees. They seem genuinely confused by every task they are asked to do. Barbara and I can only look at each other.

After a harrowing ride through the hospital – jerks and jolts and near misses – they load me into the ambulance, leaving the back door open. A small brown sparrow lands on the top of the open door, his eyes darting. He reviews the scene thoroughly, glances down at me, and disappears. No instructions. Everything seems okay.

My keepers huddle outside for yet another discussion. They allow Barbara to sit in the back with me and one of the attendants. Gauges are set, monitors consulted, and drip rates adjusted. We are off.

At the airport we pull up beside a private runway. We sit there for a long time, waiting for an ambulance plane that is coming from Pennsylvania. 'Breathe,' Barbara gently reminds me when I start to squirm around.

A blue, twin-engine ambulance plane eventually rumbles up beside the ambulance. The attendants pile out, dressed in matching blue uniforms. Another trade-off is made, the unfastening and fastening accomplished with urgent efficiency. *These guys must have the meter running.*

Where Barbara can sit is again debated, and she ultimately straps herself in beside my gurney. I am checked and re-checked, even as the pilot runs through his departure checklist. Every sign and signal is dutifully recorded, perhaps in anticipation of an insurance review. *This guy was sick and we kept him alive.*

Then we are down the runway and into the cloudless sky. I raise my head to catch a glimpse of the fleeing countryside, only to be reminded by the attendant not to strain myself. Soon we are out over Lake Michigan, sixty-five miles of cold northern blue. Barbara announces a sail below. I raise my head, but cannot see it.

'We'll be out there in no time.'

Milwaukee is sweltering when we reach the ground and taxi to the ambulance waiting on the tarmac. Another hurried consultation is convened, the exchange of records, x-rays and scans, the brisk fumbling with monitors, electrodes, intravenous bags, and tubes. A new set of attendants takes over, their soaked uniforms matted against their chests and shoulders. The wind is swirling, adding a dusty grime to all of us as they lift me out of the plane and into the ambulance. They give Barbara a narrow seat beside me.

'Turn that air conditioning up,' one barks as they clamber in, slamming the doors behind them. For reasons that escape me, they turn on the siren, weaving in and out of the intimidated rush-hour traffic.

Is this really about me?

•••••

WHO I THOUGHT I WAS HAS BEEN disappearing for a while. Now the descent begins in earnest. There is nothing to do but let go. I am set upon by a new procession of question-askers, sheet-arrangers and blood-drawers. There is a perceptible gentleness about them, a calmness about the place. They are open and unashamed of their alliance with St Francis – Francis of Assisi from the feel of it.

In the early evening I am visited by a brown-and-black-robed nun. She has that ageless quality of a true believer, a layered sweetness.

'We at St Francis want to attend to all of your needs,' she opens, 'physical, emotional and spiritual.'

'Surgery can be an opportunity to look at your life,' she continues. 'To make changes. To grow.'

I agree with every word, but feel a mounting resistance. *Let go. She wants to help.*

It is only a matter of time until she asks my religious affiliation.

'Raised a conservative Catholic,' I answer evenly, not a trace of accusation. 'My spiritual life is pretty personal, Sister,' I demur. 'Everything I was given, with more than a dash of Buddhism and Hindu mysticism.'

She smiles thinly, nods her openness and understanding. *Where do we go from here?* She seems at a loss for words.

'Have you read the Upanishads?' I ask, a sincere but thick-skulled attempt to put her at ease.

'No, I haven't,' she replies graciously. We relax down into mutism, gradually past awkwardness to warmth. We smile at each other – really smile.

'I'm a big fan of your guy, Francis,' I add, to which she further warms. Agendas are falling away. We *are* on the same team.

In the next half hour we explore common ground, conversation easy and open. As she leaves she pats the back of my hand. 'I'll be here for you, praying for you.'

'Thank you, Sister. I need all the help I can get.'

•••••

DR JERRY FRANZ SWEEPS IN NEXT, with his surgical entourage in tow. They are lean and trim, as pretty as he is not. Balding, broad-faced, comfortable with the belly that hangs over his belt, he is a force to be reckoned with. He didn't run his laps this morning – or this decade for that matter. And it wasn't white wine he was sipping last night. His gaze is direct, from eyes as mirthful as his brow is not. He could just as well be foreman of the third shift. Strong hands, thick fingers. Working man's hands, unlike a surgeon's. Hands from my old neighbourhood, or from a farm.

He is playful in a grizzly bear way. We hit it off immediately. I am soon teasing him like a long-lost friend, which seems okay until his staff enjoys my irreverence too openly. I back off quickly. This is not the time or place to be fomenting insurrection.

Jerry Franz gives as good as he gets, at one point

hoisting a well-worn boot up onto my bed, 'just so you know who you're dealing with'. He tells me to bring earplugs to surgery if I don't like country and western music. I like this guy a lot. He'll open me up on Wednesday morning, shortly after dawn.

●●●●●

AFTER BARBARA LEAVES FOR A NEARBY HOTEL, I am left with an almost eerie stillness: A quiet hospital, a staff of true believers. The intimacy of the place more than offsets any initial reservations about its small-town proportions, its lack of pretence.

Perhaps I am making peace with the inevitability of it all.

No sense spending time looking in the rearview mirror. You learn what you can and let go of the rest. What good is agonizing about what's over the horizon, for that matter?

This is it.

This empty room in an otherwise full life. A new night-shift nurse, shy and sweet. She relaxes into brief conversations, energized by the discovery that we are both runners.

Used to be a runner. It has been six months since I've run. *Maybe in the future*, out ahead of myself again.

Will I ever have eyes clear enough to recognize that everything I need is here right now?

I long to be wide awake.

●●●●●

D DAY, MINUS ONE: A blur of last-minute tasks, that most important assessment of blood flow through carotid arteries to my brain. Will intervention kill me? The man in the next bed has his urgently needed surgery put on hold because of severe blockage in his carotids. He now needs surgery before surgery, a decision he greets with limp resignation. His wife breaks down and weeps quietly. He is here a mere six months after failed surgery elsewhere. They have run out of options.

'These are the only people who will even try,' she tells me. 'Now this . . .'

Late in the afternoon they give me the green light. They will open me up tomorrow.

Barbara rolls in before noon, with several friends who have motored in for the main event. The tone of our conversation deteriorates quickly, with lavish irreverence for my fading health. The locker-room humour is welcome relief in my battle against victimhood. This is largely lost on some of the nurses, who deal out sharp glances for my most egregious tormenters.

'Laughter helps,' I assure them, but they are not buying it.

John Ryan arrives mid-afternoon, his sisters safely ensconced with friends back in Grand Rapids. We have some time alone. I want to talk about all the important things, the ones I have been harping on for years. When I make a faltering start, he quickly cuts me off.

'Dad, I know all of that. You've told me a thousand times.' With an uncharacteristic dropping of the veil, he adds, 'I've always understood what you were saying.'

'I haven't swallowed you down whole,' he continues, the beginnings of a grin, 'but enough to give me a stomach ache.'

He is looking right into me.

'We live in each other . . .' I start, my voice breaking.

'Dad, it's all right. I *know*. I'm okay, whatever happens. We cannot be apart.'

It is enough.

'I'll see you in the morning, before surgery.' Then he is gone, driving Barbara back to the hotel.

•••••

THE HALLUCINATION THAT IS OPEN-HEART SURGERY is well under way during a restless night. My nurse is aware that I am not sleeping. She gives me an early morning back rub, the magic of touch.

When she is gone I edge closer to sleep, struggling to put aside a chronic sense that I should be doing, thinking, understanding something more, wringing some fresh insight out of my situation.

I have no answers.

•••••

THE BRIGHT OVERHEAD LIGHT is not enough to wake me. 'Good morning.' A smooth hand on my forearm. 'We need to get you ready.'

'Ready' is a lot of things, the most unnerving of which involves shaving everything below my neck. *Relax, it's kind of kinky*. It is a directive I cannot follow.

Barbara and John Ryan are let in later, shadows under their bloodshot eyes. Within minutes a grim gurney team arrives, erasing the smile on Barbara's face. Drowsy now from the first sedative, I roll down the corridor in an enveloping haze. Several floors above, a nurse directs Barbara and John Ryan to a waiting room. We let go of each other's hands, and I am wheeled in the opposite direction, down into that other night.

•••••

WHEN YOU ARE AT SEA, the most interesting fog is not a night time fog. The night robs fog of some of its mystery. Nor is it a cloudy-day fog. The most interesting fog happens under a bright sun, as it is burning away. The sun amazes the fog, sets it ashimmer even as it annihilates. In these incandescent moments, you cannot see, and it is simply too beautiful for that to matter.

I emerge slowly from such a fog into the anaesthesia-softened brightness of an overhead light. Someone is standing there, a long way off, maybe more than one.

'Welcome back,' a velvet voice intones. Then everything falls away again, succumbs to the enveloping radiance.

This overhead sun works its contrary magic with time. Outlines emerge and recede. Someone is asking questions of Dr Otterbacher. He does not answer; does not even try. Later he will try, but he cannot speak. Something is in his throat.

Barbara is the first to visit me there. 'Hi, sweetheart,' followed quickly by, 'don't try to talk.' I can feel her hand on my arm, then stroking my cheek. I see what seems to be her face, but it quickly blurs, disappears.

She comes and goes as the fog burns off. She is joined by others, a male voice now, who doesn't go away. In time I can see him, dark-haired and intense, and athletic like his female colleagues. He is there when Barbara reminds me, 'You can't talk. You have a tube in your throat. Use this if you want,' handing me a pad of paper and a pencil.

She is kissing my bare forehead now, the only available place on my tube-stuffed face. I reach up and feel the tubes, prompting a 'try not to touch them' from the male voice in the room.

Still later, I scrawl a tentative 'Hi.'

'I love you,' follows in response to questions I do not comprehend – that and, 'I'm okay.'

John Ryan floats in and kisses me. 'You did great, Pops.' He has tears in his eyes. I'm sure I don't look so good. Other friends look in later.

'Pull up a chair,' I scribble.

As the worst of the fog burns off, a different burning comes on. It is centred in my chest, but extends down my shaved right leg.

When Barbara asks me if I am in pain, I write 'Yes.' I vaguely remember the stern admonitions to get medication for pain early, 'before it gets out of hand'.

Barbara talks with my nurse, then leaves the room in tears when he tells her we must wait. *The pain isn't that bad*, I want to shout after her, but I am sideswiped by the eruption in my chest when I try to raise my head. I can hear myself moaning, but I am far away again.

Time does not exist where I am, only *now*. Flickers of light as my eyes flutter, vague episodes of attention, momentary breaks in the receding fog.

Barbara remembers my macho determination not to miss tonight's televised basketball game. The nurse turns it on as Barbara leaves for her first meal of the day. It is after 8pm.

'How long was I in surgery?' I write.

'Till a little after 6pm.'

Dr Franz earned his pay today.

I cannot focus on the game, slipping in and out of consciousness. At one point I hear voices in my room.

'I don't like it,' the male voice says. 'I think we should call Dr Franz.'

I wake up later to Barbara's touch. The TV is off. She has tears in her eyes.

'What's going on – the *truth*?' I scribble woodenly, words without the feeling.

'There's too much blood in the drainage.' Barbara points to a tube protruding from between my lower ribs.

'Dr Franz is coming back,' she adds in a reassuring tone. I am not particularly reassured, but I am incapable of panic. Whatever is happening is happening.

Later someone announces, 'Dr Franz is here.' He forces a smile when our eyes meet, but does not hold it when he examines the drainage bag and consults with the nurses. There is no hint of playfulness when he announces, 'He's bleeding internally. We'll have to go back in.'

I know this isn't good, but with uncommon detachment. *Nothing I can do.*

Barbara and John Ryan are allowed back in, the five-minute restriction waived by Franz.

'They'll fix it,' I write, a limp attempt to reassure. Nods all around, but nobody's talking.

I lapse back into unconsciousness as last-minute preparations for surgery get underway, everything vague and unreal. I don't remember saying 'goodbye.'

●●●●●

I'm wheeled back into surgery at 2.20am. In the mid-morning haze from which I later emerge, someone tells me, 'You did fine.'

Barbara later explains that they found several bleeding sites after opening my chest. They repaired them, then wired and stitched me back up, 'stable but critical'.

Are we on the other side of the hill? I wonder, too tired to write it out.

'Please get some sleep,' I finally scrawl. Later, at the staff's insistence, Barbara and John Ryan leave. They promise to call her with any change in my status.

I lapse back into a deep sleep.

•••••

When I awake, I am back in ICU, a nurse assigned full-time. Nothing about her registers, only the hand and forearm that rest on the sheet beside me.

By the time Barbara and John Ryan arrive, I am having short-term episodes of clarity. I am struck by the technology that attends me. Wires trail out from under my sheets, relaying a myriad of messages to the barricade of machines around me. Needles in arms and hands, and tubes snaking off at odd angles to transparent hanging bags, they drip away in silence, their measured drops the length of my attention span. One stark wire protrudes directly from a hole in my lower chest. A drainage tube exudes from the other side.

I am an observer here, a chemical hostage to aneasthesia and pain medication. When awake, I look on with the detachment of an alien, worn out by transit through light years and dark. The room itself is from another place.

The walls are all glass. People look in at me impassively and move on.

'It's like a space station,' John Ryan observes.

When I twist my head, I can see fellow aliens in other glass compartments. They mostly look like corpses, lifeless faces white or yellow, their slack mouths and jagged noses crammed with tubes of different sizes.

'Do I look that bad?' I scribble.

'You've looked better, Dad,' John replies with unnecessary candour. I try to smile but my mouth cannot manage it. My lips purse around the emergency intubation tube in my mouth. *I could do without this damn thing.*

People come and go, skewed images mostly. I sleep as much as I can. I am very tired, more so with the passage of time. This is a lost day, a welcome hole in my conscious life.

•••••

I come back to life gradually, shackled to machinery and pain. With growing awareness comes the incessant after-ache at what they have done to me. Not just my chest and leg, but the complaint down the centre of my back, the ligaments strained as they pried open my ribs. And I can't stand this tube down my throat.

'Weren't they supposed to take it out the first day?' I write.

'The tube must stay for a while,' a nurse tells me evenly. 'A while' never gets defined to my satisfaction. The tube takes some of the pleasure out of Barbara's announcement that our girls are on their way to Milwaukee.

'I don't want the girls to see me this way,' I scribble.

Barbara understands. 'We'll hold them off until they take it out.' I nod my relief.

Friends come and go, one visit blurring into the next one. I doze intermittently, waking after dark. The lights are dimmed, the space ship still. For the first time in a long while I am alone. It feels like progress.

This thin reverie is broken when a nurse shifts in her chair beside my bed. Disappointment quickly gives way to relief as she leans over, brushes my forearm, and smiles.

'You're doing just great,' she replies to whatever question she sees in my eyes. *I am surrounded by angels.* I attempt to smile back.

•••••

WE SLIP INTO OVERDRIVE JUST AFTER DAWN, with a flurry of activity that seems like progress. The drainage from my chest cavity has dwindled, and my oxygen levels are apparently up to some standard for independence.

'Let's get those tubes out,' the day nurse announces.

'This might smart' seems like an understatement when a specialist finally gets around to the yanking. When I try to rinse the foulness from my mouth, the pain from the chest tube is overwhelmed by the inflamed rawness in my throat. My first words barely rise to the level of a whisper, the hoarse workings of a traumatized larynx. It does feel good to have those damn tubes out though, almost human.

I get my first chance to walk when Barbara arrives. It is a welcome but unsteady performance. The hard part is lifting myself out of bed and onto my feet. Stitches from ankle to neck complain at any point where effort and stretching intersect. *Feels like somebody chopped me up*, the irony obscured by the pain.

When Barbara winces at my discomfort, I whisper, 'You ought to see the other guy.' But there is no other guy, no opponent to blame or pummel. I am in the ring alone. If I am on the mat, a turgid mix of genetics and life pace put me there.

I *have* thrown myself around a bit.

After an abbreviated shuffle down the corridor, Barbara and I begin to plot a strategy for recovery. I want to *make* myself better. She reminds me that pushing too hard will slow my recovery, maybe even shorten my life.

I know she's right. 'Slow down' needs to become more than a slogan. This is a hard one for me, because it feels like a concession. I'm not that good at concessions, even necessary ones.

My prime motivators arrive in a pony-legged flurry in mid-afternoon. John Ryan has warned Katie and Erin what to expect. He stands behind them, rubbing their shoulders, easing them through their initial shock. Soon they are up on the bed, peppering me with questions, telling me excitedly about their latest adventures. They bring with them an almost gravitational pull into the future, theirs and mine. I want to go there with them, as far as I possibly can.

●●●●●

LATER, WHEN I AM ALONE, I remember a favourite Joseph Campbell quote:

> 'The goal is to live
> with godlike composure
> on the full rush of energy,
> like Dionysus riding the leopard,
> without being torn to pieces.'

I replay it over and over, edging towards sleep. *Composure is going to take some practice.*

• • • • •

BARBARA AND THE GIRLS LEAVE A DAY LATER. We have celebrated Father's Day as best we can, taking several long strolls together. I want them back in Grand Rapids before dark, a weak attempt to provide a security I can no longer assure. Barbara leaves with difficulty. Nothing I can say seems to help much, but I try.

'I'll be just behind you. Johnny will keep me in line.'

'I know he will,' she replies, finally smiling. His new-found paternalism amuses both of us, coming as it does after years of general mayhem.

'I'd just like to be with you,' she adds.

'You are,' and she is gone, the girls with her.

• • • • •

LATER, ON A SAUNTER DOWN THE HALL, I run into Dr Franz. I answer his questions, then ask him to sit down on a bench near the window.

'I know you're very busy, Jerry – and that part of your job is doling out encouragement. But I need some real straight talk. Will you do that for me?'

Discomfort spreads across his broad face. He nods gruffly, glances away, then squints directly at me.

'So tell me, how's my heart?

'The *truth*,' I add firmly when he hesitates.

'Your heart is a bit of a mess, John. It's not good. But you seem to have a powerhouse will to live. I've seen how you and Barbara are around each other . . .' His voice trails off.

'I'll do anything to live,' I want to reassure him, aware of the spot I've put him in. 'But my heart is pretty sick,' less a question than a statement.

'It's pretty sick.'

Most of my other questions suddenly seem unimportant.

'Anything more I can do?' I want to give him a way out.

'You're already doing everything I could ask.' Looking directly at me now, 'Go out there and surprise us.'

'I plan to.'

Our consultation is over. As we stand up, I grab his arm. 'I can never thank you enough – *whatever* happens – for taking me on, for what you've done for me and my family.'

'Go out there and surprise us,' he repeats, with a weary smile. When I say nothing, he turns and lumbers down the hall.

• • • • •

THEY KEEP ME FOR TWO MORE DAYS THAT FEEL LIKE TEN, and finally release me on the condition that I stay at a nearby hotel for a few more days.

John Ryan helps me take a shower before we leave. I

don't want him to see me carved up like this. He tries to disguise his squeamishness with toughness. 'They messed you up, big boy.'

Shortly after we arrive at the hotel – T-shirt, shorts, and a single white surgical stocking – I insist on going out.

'I'm tired of being cooped up. I'm *not* going to overdo it.' I feel like an adolescent, begging his father for the car keys.

John eventually relents, much as his father often has. Soon we are making our way through suburban Milwaukee, heat radiating off the truck's bonnet.

'A little slower, please,' when a bump sets off pain in my fissures.

'Sorry, Dad.' His meekness underlines how vulnerable I have become.

'Let's see if we can find a good bookshop,' I suggest, shifting away from our awkward role reversal.

We find a sprawling superstore in a suburban shopping centre. Next to the bookshop is an equally faceless department store. I miss the girls, and want to buy them souvenirs to take the edge off their Milwaukee experience.

'Let's stop in here and look around.'

We push our way through the swinging doors. The air conditioning, a welcome affront, calls up the frigidity of the surgical units. We find what we are looking for in sporting goods, a couple of T-shirts celebrating the local franchise. When I reach down to pick up a matching pair of shorts, I lose my balance, can't right or protect myself, and lurch into John. Although he keeps me from falling down completely, the damage is done. I have stretched the stitches in my chest and leg.

I gasp at the pain of it, even more at the despair over what I have become. I thank John through gritted teeth, then cave in, choking on resentment and hopelessness. Embarrassed, I thrust the shirts at him to purchase.

'Oh, damn!' he stammers at the look on my face.

'I'll be at the truck,' pulling away from him and limping stiffly towards the door. My reserve cracks when I get outside. I stand by the truck sobbing, trying to hold my head above the lapping horror of it all.

We sit in the truck for a long time, the engine on, air conditioning vents aimed at the blood spots appearing on my shirt and surgical hose. John wants to go back to the hospital, or at least to the hotel. I use what little authority I have left to convince him to stay where we are. The bleeding will stop on its own, I argue, energy returning in the form of resolve. *Get back up*.

'I'm sorry to put you through this, John.'

'You haven't *put* me through anything,' he snaps back. 'Why don't you cut yourself some slack?'

I sit there dumb and nodding, a wave of resignation that takes me by surprise: 'I would really like to go in the bookshop. Just sit and read for a while, have a cup of coffee.'

'Are you *sure*?' John's off balance.

'Yes, I am.'

After a long pause, he reaches up and turns off the engine, handing me back my dignity: 'You tell me if it gets to be too much.'

•••••

WE STOP AT THE OLIVE GARDEN after the bookshop, have an early dinner to celebrate my emancipation. Halfway through a salad, the pain is taking over. John hurriedly gets his dinner boxed, and we leave.

Back at the hotel I go in the bathroom, pour a glass of water, and swallow down a pain pill. I begin a second glass of water. I stand in front of the mirror, waiting for the relief that will only come later. I reach back and push the door shut.

'Are you okay in there?' John is right up against the door.

'Yeah, I am,' easing the door open to show him. 'I've just got to go to the bathroom.'

'You shout if there's anything I can do,' he relents, walking back into the room.

With the door closed behind me, I step up to the mirror again. It's like looking at a stranger. The time in the hospital – the drugs, the cutting, the institutional food – have taken fifteen pounds off me. I am gaunt and grey-faced, a tinge of yellow under my eyes. Dull, empty eyes, devoid of any recognizable life. *Who is this man?*

I reach down to pull off my T-shirt. Try as I might, I can't do it. I hike it up far enough to see the clotted line of stitches stretching from the top of my stomach up towards my throat, arching slightly towards the left.

'What a mess,' an almost reassuring burst of intensity. 'What an ugly mess.'

I feel like crying, but the tears do not come. Instead bile rises in my throat, a spasm in my diaphragm. I choke back a convulsion and drop my shirt. I grip the sink with both hands, my equilibrium slipping away, trying to reconnect with something solid in myself. *Get back up.*

John is at the door again, tapping softly. 'You okay,

Dad?' He opens the door a crack to look in. Our glances lock in the mirror, my distress exposed.

'I've been better.'

●●●●●

JOHN AND I MAKE ANOTHER TENTATIVE VENTURE the next day. The heat drives us into the uncomfortable chill of another bookshop. I try to capture what I am experiencing in words, then crumple up the paper in frustration. I am too sodden with anaesthesia and pain killers to sustain a line of thought. Muteness compounds my sense of unreality.

Like a wounded animal, I simply want to go home. John does his best to turn our hotel room into a crash pad, a clutter-strewn approximation of road trips we have made over the years. I retreat into the drivel of TV, no thought required. I doze off when I can, assuring myself that every hour of sleep takes me closer to recovery. Mostly it is relief from terrain I am unable to navigate.

I am in and out of sleep during the night. I awake to a nightmare of confusion and pain, the profound sense of being less than I was before, damaged goods. I resent wanting the relief medication offers. I want to be whole and well. Now.

Deal with what is, I tell myself over and over. *You are in control of how you respond to this*. The words sound thin and hollow. *Grace* seems out of reach.

●●●●●

THE INNER DELIRIUM PERSISTS during a tortured drive back to Grand Rapids, then swamps the first week home. I struggle to reclaim some semblance of normality. I go to the health club within days of arrival, determined to re-discover strength and vigour. I walk on the treadmill for half an hour, then shower with relief in an empty locker room. I am not ready to be seen naked yet, to expose myself to friends' strained assurances. Afterwards I pay the price. Pain cuts me in half, and sends me to bed early.

I meet with my first clients the following week, a bravado-laden gesture of resilience. Their concern helps. What I bring to the table is less certain, my vapour-laden brain incapable of subtlety.

Everywhere I turn I am met with kindness, the sincerity of which seems undeniable. I try to accept it at face value, an offset against discouragement. Off the medication after a week, I am racked with pain and impatience. I remind myself that recovery happens at its own pace. This is a river I cannot push.

* * * * *

Barbara drives us to Whitehall on my first weekend home, back to Crosswinds Marina where *Grace* is tied to a dock. I pull myself up over her lifelines in a spasm, and sit down in the cockpit. It has been just two weeks since I locked up the companionway for the night, excited about the prospect of summer's first sail on the following day. Two weeks and a lifetime ago, a hefty toolbox in either hand. I can hardly believe this is real.

Grace is real. I look her over, fresh appreciation for her teak deck and varnished coamings, her rakish over-hang, and powerhouse rig. She rocks just perceptibly in the afternoon lull, a liquid reminder of what she does in open water. I can *feel* her, the beginnings of a smile.

'Happy?'

'Yup, feels good to be back.'

Later, over dinner, 'I still want to go out there.'

'So do I.' Nothing more.

'I've got almost a year to get better. If things are going to go haywire, we'll know by then.'

'Things aren't going to go haywire, John. You've just got to heal up, get strong again.'

'Then we'll go,' a question within the statement.

'Then we'll go,' she smiles back.

●●●●●

THINGS DON'T GO SIDEWAYS RIGHT AWAY.

It takes four weeks.

On a morning walk in mid-July, I first notice the pressure building in my chest. Deep inside, beneath the surface scar tissue, beneath the mending tendons and returning muscle, down closer to the centre, where there never has been any surgical burn, the first vague suggestion of an ache. *I'm imagining this*, I tell myself. When the pain doesn't go away, I resort to stern denial: *You're becoming a hypochondriac.*

I pick up the tempo. *This is only a cramp. Walk through it.* But I can't walk through it. It intensifies with my pace, broadens and swells, filling up my chest. I reach in my pocket for the bottle of nitro I haven't touched since surgery. I slip a tablet beneath my tongue and slow my pace, a concession to the deepening pain.

I don't want the nitro to help. If it doesn't cut into the ache, it's probably not my heart. When there is no immediate relief, I renew my pace in hopeful defiance. *It's not my heart.* But even as I say it, there is a settling beneath my sternum, a slight but real relaxation in the pressure. My spirit sags even as the pain recedes. The pain responds to nitro. *Can it be my heart?* It's only been a month since surgery. *How can it be my heart?*

Exercise is over for the day. I walk slowly back home. I tell no one, not even Barbara. It may be a fluke, and I don't want to trouble her over a fluke. I'll give it another go tomorrow.

•••••

IT IS NOT A FLUKE.

It comes to get me halfway into next morning's walk. So faint at first that I can tell myself it's not real, it intensifies as I hold my pace. It gives way to the bitterness of a nitro tablet beneath my tongue. *It's back.* They have fixed me, but I am not fixed.

After work, after dinner and the ritual of getting the girls to bed, I tell Barbara. She is absolutely still, anchored to the bed. She doesn't speak, doesn't even seem to breathe. It is the wave she didn't see coming. She is submerged, unreachable. After a long time, 'Are you sure?'

'I'd love to be wrong.'

'I'm so sorry,' then she convulses into tears.

'So am I.'

•••••

WE MEET RICK WITHIN DAYS. He peppers me with questions, unwilling to believe that this is happening. I feel chagrined when he recites less dire alternatives, as if I have let us down somehow. I am desperate for anything that will undermine my suspicions, but nothing he suggests rings true.

Finally, reluctantly, I ask, 'What if this is for real, Rick? What if it is my heart?'

Rick – who always has an answer, always an idea or a 'then we'll . . .' – pulls up short. There is something new in his eyes, in the way his lips purse and the skin tightens over his cheekbones. Is it fear? His response, after a long pause, does not satisfy.

'I think we're a long way from having to worry about that, John.' He looks at Barbara, but she is looking down. 'Let's keep a close eye on this, and see if it goes away. I wouldn't be surprised if it does.'

Later, getting into the car and reaching for the seat belt, Barbara says out loud what we're both thinking. 'That wasn't very reassuring.'

'No, it wasn't.' I stare numbly into the underbrush beyond the car park.

•••••

JULY WINDS DOWN LIKE a truce that will not hold.

I move with hesitation through the details of daily life. I get the kids off to camp, see clients, catch up with friends over lunch. I try to touch every base, but I am sleepwalking, fending off discouragement. I spend long nights looking out the windows which encircle our bed, at the trees and the moon, trying not to wake Barbara. She jokingly refers to my postoperative insomnia as 'sleeping with a new-born'.

Only total exhaustion affords relief from the uncertainty embedded in the night, my fitful episodes of sleep punctuated by spasmodic awakenings. Even the best dreams veer off. In flight, I am unable to avoid the overhanging wires.

The pressure in my chest returns with every exercise session, which I complete with the help of nitro. It shows up when Barbara and I make love, which I refuse to relinquish. I furtively slip a nitro under my tongue on the way to bed. The ache will fade away afterwards. What doesn't leave me is growing certainty that something – in spite of all assurances, all my best efforts – is wrong. The jagged incision in my chest is healing, but my heart is not.

At the end of the month I go back to the hospital for another Thallium stress test. It confirms what my heart has been telling me for weeks. The blood is not getting to the left ventricle, the pump house, sending it into the irregular spasms I experience as weakness, pressure and pain. I am back at the brink of a major heart attack.

'You were right, John,' Rick is almost apologetic when he delivers the news.

'I'd rather not have been right.'

'We've got to go back in – again – to see what's going on.' When we say nothing, he adds, 'I'm sorry.'

'When?' Barbara asks.

'Waiting could be dangerous. I'd like to do it as soon as possible.'

'That's okay with me,' I nod at Barbara.

'There's nothing worse than not knowing,' with less conviction than I intend.

We stare at each other in silence. We are out of words.

●●●●●

For the seventh time in seven months, they roll me into surgery. I am numb to a routine for which I can normally muster a sour blend of loathing and fear. The first technician fails to find a vein, giving way to the equally futile attempts of her stand-in. Blood runs down my forearm, dripping off my fingers onto the floor. Incapable of my usual agitation, I look on like a bystander. Barbara tries to hide the horror on her face.

Rick enters the cold inner sanctum with his usual good nature.

'You okay?'

I nod, not wanting to lie out loud. 'What's the alternative?'

Rick gives my arm a supportive squeeze. We have been reduced to sign language.

The curtain drops mercifully with the first injection.

●●●●●

'We've got the LAD open.' Rick is back on track, relief overriding whatever post-surgical weariness he feels. 'I put another stent in there. Blood flow looks good.'

'What happens if it closes up again, Rick, next week, or a month from now?' I want to add, 'like everything else has,' but I know it will sound like an attack. Agitation feels better than fear.

Rick's face hardens somewhat, as if he heard what I didn't say. He pauses, unwilling to escalate.

'Your heart won't pump without the muscle the LAD feeds,' he says evenly, then lets it sink in. 'I don't think it's helpful to go there.'

When Barbara and I say nothing, Rick adds, 'The LAD was the worst,' as if he can slip it by us.

'The worst?' When he doesn't reply immediately, I press him.

'What about the rest?'

'None of it looks that good.' This is clearly not a conversation he wants.

I look over at Barbara, sensing instinctively where not to go. We are running on fumes as it is. This is all we can handle. I have survived again, exhausted but stable. Stop the bleeding. Pile on more sandbags if you must. Give me something to help me sleep my way back to natural energy. If not that, at least enough that I dare to see our children tonight.

•••••

RICK'S SURGICAL SUMMARY COVERS THE GROUND we didn't discuss. After detailing the critical blockages in the LAD, he continues: 'This is a very small distal Circumflex. The vein graft to the Circumflex is somewhat tortuous and has a 40% proximal narrowing.'

The report on the Right Coronary Artery reads like a bullet: 'RCA: Severe diffuse disease.'

Rick is right in not going into it with us. There is a place where honesty becomes piling it on.

Barbara and I are choking on the small portion we have pressured out of him.

•••••

I FEEL ALMOST HUMAN BY THE TIME the day nurse glides in, a saccharine 'Good morning, John.'

The bleeding has stopped. Something has decayed in my mouth. 'I need to brush my teeth.'

Within an hour I am given clearance to move around, to confront that first sustained look in the mirror.

Barbara arrives early. I am determined that she take Katie and Erin for their annual overnight camping trip with their Aunt Audrey and their cousin, Ben.

'I really want to go, but I feel lousy about leaving you here.'

'I'm getting out of here this afternoon. Ric and Dan are going to take me sailing. We've already talked about all of this.' How to stand firm without lapsing into impatience.

'I know, but . . .'

'No buts about it. This is a big deal for the girls. They *deserve* a big deal. So do you.

'I'll have a great time with the guys – my first sail of the year. We'll link up down at Saugatuck tomorrow night, and begin our holiday there.'

'It's about time,' she relents without further protest.

•••••

RIC MILLER PICKS ME UP SHORTLY AFTER NOON.

My oldest friend, we first met in a neighbourhood alley when I was five. A long stint as a marketing executive has done little damage to his underlying decency and playfulness. During the car ride out to the marina, Ric listens while I admit to discouragement. By the time we reach Whitehall, we are beyond that, laughing heartily at each other's expense. Dan joins us aboard *Grace* within the hour.

Like all close friends, Ric and Dan can be counted on

for anything but reverence. Their disdain for my fragility is exactly what I need.

'I remember when you could raise the sails by yourself, before you got old and lame.'

'After all the crap you've been peddling about *us* staying healthy . . .'

We ease *Grace* out of her slip, into the open water.

'Is *steering* too much for you?'

It is August. I am finally going sailing.

By sunset we are gliding down the east coast of Lake Michigan. We will spend the night at Grand Haven, a port town twenty miles south of Whitehall. Although it has been seven weeks since my open-heart surgery, time at the helm awakens pain in my chest. *Just stretching the scar tissue*, I tell myself. When the throbbing in my groin kicks in, I sag down on a cockpit cushion. I don't want to break open the new incision.

'Remember when we couldn't pry him off the wheel?'

Dan shakes his head in mock disbelief. 'Long time ago . . .'

These two will cut me no slack. It's a ritual refined over decades together: shared losses and wins, romances, divorces, hopes and fears about children, successes and heartaches of every kind. A brotherhood where antagonism and respect are indistinguishable. Although I have long revelled in a reputation for going the distance, nothing is said when I excuse myself early to go back to the boat during dinner. We all know it is different now. Dan takes the edge off my early departure as I get to the door:

'He's probably got Barbara stowed away in his cabin.'

• • • • •

RIC HEADS OFF TO WORK IN THE MORNING. After dallying over the sports page at breakfast, Dan and I wander back to *Grace*. The sun is a warm reprieve after the confinement of the hospital. I am thankful for everything: the off-centre smile of our waitress, the crooning of an unseen cook, the texture of the grass when I kick off my boat shoes. I sprawl on the lawn next to the dock, spewing Whitman as Dan climbs up over the lifelines, looking to escape.

'There was never any more inception than there is now . . .'

I stretch until the seams complain, roll side to side like a dog. I feel almost human, almost carefree.

'and will never be any more perfection than there is now . . .'

Dan looks on with scorn.
'You expect me to be bowled over by that poetry crap just because you're at death's door?'

● ● ● ● ●

LATE IN THE AFTERNOON A NORTHWESTERLY kicks in with unexpected gusto, the sky sunny and clueless. Dan and I go into a sail-trimming routine we have refined over many years, only to struggle with a tangled, uncooperative genoa. After a long and poorly coordinated effort, we finally tame the beast.
'That wasn't pretty.'
'It'd help if I could carry my weight,' my impatience tinged with self-pity.

'Get over it,' he says evenly.

'Thank you,' I reply, after a moment's consideration.

The sun ripens to August proportions as we approach the breakwater at Saugatuck. I reluctantly pull off my sweat-soaked shirt. No one outside the family has seen the harsh carving on my chest.

Dan, seasoned veteran of mayhem on and off the athletic field, winces when he sees what they've done.

'Yikes! Those boys had a go at you.'

'Yes, they did,' struggling not to be ashamed of what I have become.

'Don't women find scars sexy?' I counter, an attempt to diffuse our discomfort.

'Yeah, but you might have gone overboard this time.'

• • • • •

BARBARA AND THE GIRLS JOIN US AT THE MARINA, a high-spirited collage of bare feet, sunburned cheeks and freckled noses. We are together on *Grace* again, in an unfamiliar harbour. We celebrate this minor accomplishment with awkward awareness that it is such a big deal for us. Everything is brand new, I remind myself, trying to find a positive angle.

Dan will sail with us back to Grand Haven. If we feel comfortable with my condition, he will leave us there. We will sail back to Whitehall alone after a week of rest.

The trip to Grand Haven turns out to be an effortless sail, a mild reassurance that Barbara and I can handle *Grace* by ourselves. We refuse Dan's offer to stay, deeply appreciative of the easy way he has accommodated us.

'I'll call if we need help,' I lie. I am determined to take this next step by ourselves. We need some victories in this most difficult year. We need momentum if we are to have any hope of leaving next summer.

• • • • •

WE REST AND LANGUISH FOR A STEAMY WEEK, pulled along by the girls' exuberance. They have not lost their verve during summer's long medical march. Being together on *Grace* is pure fuel indeed. They burn brightly from morning to night. Barbara and I soak up their enthusiasm in the sweet sexy ambience of bare skin and beach walks. We are trying to establish new footings, to reconnect with native energy.

We make unsteady attempts to inject optimism into the uncertainty with which we live. Shorts, sandals and halter tops help, as does the cautious rediscovery of sex. In spite of my latest incisions, we move comfortably on this terrain.

I am still too sore to test my heart with sustained exercise. We want to believe I am healing, not just outside, but inside. Our spirits gradually rise with each day further from the hospital.

'We can do this' we remind each other as the week winds down. We begin making plans to take *Grace* back to Whitehall.

• • • • •

ON THE MORNING BEFORE WE ARE DUE TO LEAVE, a sailing friend rouses us out of sleep with an invitation to join him for breakfast. Elwin Ruehs is a welcome sight, even for squinting eyes. Warm and understated, he loves to laugh. He also loves to wallow in our shared passion for long-distance sailing. We are members of a small fraternity of

Great Lakes sailors who have found their way out to the ocean for extended cruises. He has been back behind a desk for too long, and is here to share a draught or two of saltwater, to brainstorm that next outlandish enterprise.

I pull on my clothes excitedly, and meet him on the dock.

'There's a good coffee shop up the street,' I announce, and give him a hearty hug. Halfway up the road I can feel the first faint stirrings of pain in my chest.

'Damnit, Elwin, I've got to slow down.' I reach for the bottle of nitro in my pocket. I try to relax as the bitterness spreads under my tongue. *Breathe through it.*

Elwin doesn't overreact when I wave off his offer of assistance. The alarm is in his uneasy sideward glances as we walk slowly up the street, in silence.

By the time we reach the counter, I am feeling some relief.

We order coffee – 'Make mine decaf, please' – and find a table.

'Does this happen often?' he asks cautiously.

'First time since my last angioplasty . . . a full ten days ago.'

'Ten days ago? I hadn't heard . . .'

After a long silence he restarts, 'I'm sorry, John. I thought the open-heart surgery had fixed all that.'

'So did I, Elwin.' I glance out of the window, then back to him, 'It didn't.'

'Damn.'

'Got that right.'

After another awkward pause, I try to reassert some normality into our conversation. Questions about his life,

Mary and the kids, and plans to go back out cruising. My attention diverts back to my chest when the pain comes on again, this time with a vengeance. Elwin notices my distress even before I reach for the nitro.

'Hurting?'

'Hurting like hell this time.'

'What do you want me to do?'

I have a pill out now, slipping it under my tongue.

'Should I get Barbara?' He is starting to get out of his chair. I reach over and grab his forearm, signalling him to stay. We sit silently, looking at each other, waiting for the nitro to deliver relief.

The surging ache overwhelms the nitro. I slip a second tablet under my tongue. It buys me some relief.

'Let's get out of here.'

'Are you sure?'

I answer by standing up. I hold the table for a moment to steady myself, then gesture towards the nearest door. Elwin walks helplessly ahead of me, pushing the door open.

The ache is ratcheting up again as we move into a corridor, still empty at this hour. It is squeezing the breath out of me.

'I need to sit down.' I slide onto a bench, then lie down.

'Please get Barbara.' I reach for another nitro.

Elwin sprints down the hall and around the corner.

The pain and pressure are spreading now, up into my neck, down into my arm. I take another nitro, fighting back the overwhelming sense of inevitability. There is no stopping this, no fixing it. I have worked hard to do the right things, to keep my spirits up. All the needles and cutting and stitching, all the exercise, and nothing seems to help.

This thing has a life of its own. It is intent on taking me from Barbara and the kids. There is nothing I can do.

'Excuse me, sir, are you okay?' A young man is standing over me, gesturing frantically to an older man who emerges from a shop.

'No, I am not okay,' in a voice so subdued I hardly recognize it. 'But help is on the way.'

'What is it?' The older man is here now, his voice softening when he sees my face.

'I'm having a problem. My heart.'

'I'll call an E-Unit,' he announces and heads back towards his shop.

'No, please, let's wait a few minutes and see if it passes.'

He is ready to argue his case when Barbara sprints in, Elwin behind her. She is down on her knees beside me.

'How bad, baby?'

'Pretty bad. Worst ever.'

'Let's get an ambulance.' The manager heads back towards his shop.

All I can think of is the chaos and confusion of an unknown patient in a small-town hospital. And the kids, exposed to the terror of it, shuttled to the side, with no friends to stand in.

'No, let's not,' I say with more authority than I feel. 'I want to go to Grand Rapids – where they know me, where Rick is – and I want to go with the kids, to get them ready.'

'Are you sure?' Barbara is scared. She wants help now.

'I think so. Please get the car and the kids. Pull it right up to the door. We'll be there in 45 minutes.'

'But if your heart stops before then . . .' Barbara's words trail off.

'I don't think it will.' I look her in the eyes. 'I want you to drive me to Grand Rapids.'

We are on the road in minutes, my seat reclined so that I can hold the girls' hands in the back. I try to reassure them, to ease the fear out of their taut faces. They have been through too much. It adds to the ache in my chest.

The pressure intensifies for minutes on end, then eases for a while. I use nitro as we ride, multiple pills to ward off the most dangerous surges. I try to focus on the here and now, to lay aside the crushing discouragement I feel. *Just get to the hospital without blowing up.*

I can't see outside, only Barbara's profile and the riveted eyes of the kids. I tell them over and over that I am going to be okay. My brain ranges from frantic obsessing to dreamy, thoughtless states, life reduced to slow motion. How the sun feels on my forearm, the elegant fragility of the girls' fingers.

When I am not fending off a convulsion or fumbling with mental logistics, I relax down into Barbara's tanned neck and arms, her freckles, the soft insistence of a breast against her T-shirt.

I don't live for grand causes, but for the abundant comforts of home. For what there is between us.

• • • • •

When we arrive at the emergency room, I clutch the kids goodbye, then surrender to the inevitable. Even the hated needles don't rile me. I am untouchable, out beyond the commotion. Barbara's eyes call me into momentary focus, then bless my sliding away. We are okay. That is all that matters.

Rick enters the circle at some point. 'You again!' he smiles.

'I haven't missed you a bit,' I reply hoarsely.

He gets right to business. 'I've got to go in again, take a look.'

'I know. We'll talk when you're done.'

'Be okay,' his hand tightens on my shoulder.

'She won't let me be anything else,' nodding at Barbara.

Within minutes I am back in the icebox of surgery. The brilliant overhead lights, the midsummer suntans of the blue-garbed nurses, the injection. That stillness beyond thought and time.

• • • • •

It must be dinnertime: there's a clatter of trays in the corridor and the uniform aroma of hospital food.

Barbara enters the room, her eyes softening when she finds me awake. Behind her comes Rick, surprisingly fresh after a day in surgery. The boy could use some sun.

'I'm glad you're awake.' He moves up to the bed where Barbara has already entwined herself. 'I wanted to talk with both of you.

'I wish I had better news . . .'

• • • • •

Barbara sits on the bed long after Rick leaves. Our hands and eyes speak when words fail us.

The bad news is that my LAD is gone for good. It is not coming back. It is totally blocked, withered to the point of uselessness. It is irreparable. My heart is now being fed by two rather than three arteries. The critical muscle of the left ventricle pumphouse has no ostensible supply of blood.

Blood tests show some enzyme 'leakage', a signal that my heart has sustained damage.

'Doesn't look *that* bad,' Rick has assured us.

More ominously, the surgically repaired circumflex artery is thoroughly diseased also, with significant blockage growing in the two-month-old vein graft. Although Rick doesn't say it directly, it is inconceivable that I will survive closure of a second artery. And whatever is closing these arteries seems to be rampaging on, unabated.

For all its innate hardiness, my heart is running on empty.

The good news – 'amazing' Rick called it – is that tiny collateral arteries seem to be springing up throughout my heart's musculature, as if anticipating the loss of my larger cardiac arteries. No substitute for the ample supply of blood that is dying away, these hair-like collaterals are providing just enough blood to keep my heart alive. The overarching danger is that the remaining Circumflex and RCA arteries – from which these collaterals are getting their blood supply – will continue to deteriorate. If they do, a terminal heart attack is unavoidable.

Our only remaining hope is for a spontaneous end to the acute, faceless disease which has for eight months ravaged these arteries. It has killed the LAD. It now threatens the remaining two coronary arteries. It must stop if I am to survive. It must stop, and the spontaneous growth of these tiny collaterals must continue, staving off starvation in the otherwise bloodless portions of my heart.

It is a narrow place to stand. Barbara and I huddle there, weary and discouraged, arms around each other.

•••••

IF YOU FALL FAR ENOUGH, it's hard to know when you hit bottom. The air gets sucked out of you on the way down. Is the lightness in your head a blessing or a curse?

Rick first broaches the subject of a heart transplant in the early afternoon of my third day in the hospital. Have I hit bottom, or is this just another level of descent?

For a moment I can't inhale. The medicinal haze in my brain seems even thicker.

'We're running out of options, aren't we?' is the best I can do.

I have trouble looking Rick in the face. He moves away from the windowsill against which he is leaning, to a place beside my bed. A chair barks as he pulls it up to sit. His silence reminds me of my respect for his refusal to sugar-coat.

Our eyes lock, with none of the usual playfulness.

'Yes, we are,' he finally replies.

He waits for it to register.

'Nothing we've tried has worked very well.' I am struggling to pay attention to his words. 'And we are out of easy options.'

'Easy?'

Rick breaks into an awkward smile. 'You didn't think open-heart surgery was easy?'

'Piece of cake,' I relax into a forgiving smile of my own. *I love this guy.*

'What I'm trying to say – if you'd let me – is that we've got to stop your free-fall somehow, until they can make a breakthrough in gene therapy or laser surgery, or something.'

'And if we can't?'

'Then we get you in line for a heart transplant.'

'How long a line?'

'It's pretty long.'

Someone is sucking the remaining air out of the room. There is nothing to say, no air with which to say it anyway.

'I haven't been a very good patient,' I finally muster, trying to take him off the hook.

He smiles wryly, then exhales. 'And we haven't been able to fix this, John. I'm sorry. But we're not going to give up.' As much a question as a statement.

'No, Rick, I'm sure as hell not going to give up.' A little too tough.

After a while he asks, 'Any other questions, for now?'

'No, it's pretty clear. Thanks – for everything you've done, and for being straight with me.'

I grab his hand in a playful shake. We have given each other absolution.

As he reaches the door, I call him back. 'Let me tell Barbara.'

'Sure,' he nods and is gone, pulling the door shut behind him.

●●●●●

I AM ALONE.

The antiseptic-laden air settles. It is as still as a hospital can be. Only the metronome of clicks from the vital sign monitors behind me. A life reduced to blips and bleeps.

I wince as a somewhat mechanical attempt to rearrange my sheets launches a jagged pain upwards from a needle in my wrist. This tube for the medications I am mainlining.

This for the drip, drip, drip of feeding and flushing fluids. Maybe the right mix will stabilize me.

Someone hollers for a nurse, ignoring the button clipped to every bedspread. Is he scared, like me? Life out of control, like me?

Perhaps we control what matters least. We grasp and grapple to manage the smallest events, pay the mortgage and change the oil. We drape ourselves in the illusion of security, even as someone loves us or ceases to, the truck meanders across the road, cancer percolates to life in a child. 'What would you like for dinner tonight?' the dietician asks. The universe decides the rest.

The room alternately ignites and darkens as a cloud surge plays with the sunlight that slants through the windows. Awash in a cross-current of feeling, I flounder, incapable of clarity or conclusion. The thought of our children growing up without their father gives me a single, terrible torrent to ride.

Life

'The morning breeze
has secrets to tell you.
Do not go back to sleep.'

– Rumi

IT WAS FRITZ PERLS, I think, who suggested that 'it is not easy to die and be born again'. It is challenging enough to go to the edge of death and set up camp there.

The second half of August is an encampment on the fields of death. I leave the hospital on tippy-toes, my life hanging on a labyrinth of tiny collaterals. The ache in my chest is an ever-available reminder that a single step beyond their frail capacity will trigger an explosion in my heart. It is an explosion I am unlikely to survive.

Barbara and the kids weave a cocoon around me at home, reminding everyone who visits that overextension is the enemy. I am in no real danger of overdoing anything. I carry a monitor in my chest. It goes off as I shuffle between bed and bathroom, underlining my limits with pain. It tells me with deadly clarity to slow down. My life depends on it.

I take handfuls of medicine each day. I am mainlining an oral form of nitroglycerin, slow-acting and constant, urging the surviving vessels to stay open. Other medicines thin my blood and inhibit its capacity to clot. Still others curtail my heart's ability to beat rapidly. I am a latter-day chemistry shop, with blood like a haemophiliac. Be careful with the Gillette.

What medication can't do is retool my intransigent, blue collar orientation: *If there's a problem, solve it; something broke, fix it. Try harder. Just do it.* My engine revs quickly in the face of challenge, up beyond the red line where a toll is paid. I have tried to fix my heart, and I have failed. I long for something tangible I can do, something I can put my hands on. I cannot reach my heart, cannot massage it back to health.

I am in new territory. After a lifetime of charging the barricades, 'acceptance' and 'surrender' are words in a foreign tongue, language I emotionally equate with capitulation.

'You love challenges, John. How about accepting what you *can't* do?' That Barbara is right is small consolation.

• • • • •

AUGUST WINDS DOWN, one inexorable day at a time. My heart doesn't blow up, although any effort yields pain. The ache that erupts when I am at rest frightens me the most. It often comes during the night, waking me out of that thin delirium I call sleep.

Daytime has a sleep-like quality to it also. Everything occurs in a haze, a rancid blend of discouragement and anesthesia. 'One month to recover from each hour you have been under' is what they told me at the hospital. I am looking at a year of this.

The early hours of the morning are the worst. I lie in bed as motionless as possible, trying to afford Barbara some uninterrupted sleep. A trooper throughout this long march, she is finally relaxing, enough to be truly exhausted.

Restless and depressed, I stare out of our bedroom windows, up through the trees to the moon. I am aware with a desperate clarity that I must *choose* to live, choose and choose again. I will die otherwise. I must *will* to live, at least enough to offset the force field into which I have slipped. Saddened at what has been lost, I must choose. In pain, or terrified, I must choose.

I *will* live, in whatever shambled state I am left.

During the day, tottering slowly about the house, I marshal all the reasons to carry on: John Ryan, Katie and Erin; friends that I relish; an animal loyalty to ageing parents and re-discovered siblings. Adventures that beckon. The ongoing romance that ripens with Barbara, her collarbones, the mystery of a sidelong glance.

'So what do you think?' she asks dreamily.

'I think we're going to get through this.'

'Of course we are.'

'You can say "of course", but I have to struggle – *choose* – to believe it.'

'I know that. I didn't mean to imply . . .' her voice trails off.

'It's okay,' I interject. 'But I can only take *not dying* so far. It's not enough for the long haul.'

'I'm glad you're thinking "long haul,"' she smiles.

'I need to *live*, not just *survive*.'

'You won't get an argument from me. What do you have in mind?'

'Sailing. Packing up the kids and taking off next summer.' There, I said it.

Barbara's face goes blank for a moment. No expression, not a word. Then, a tentative 'What if you're not able?'

'If I don't pull out of this, I'll be dead long before summer.' Full steam ahead. 'If I'm alive come summer, I'll be better, well enough to go.'

Barbara listens. I don't have a clue what she's thinking.

'I hope you've got more reasons to live than just our trip,' she finally says. *Our* trip.

'Of course I do. You, the kids. I love our life . . .'

Neither of us says anything for a while, a silence like death.

'Listen, I know this is a long shot, but I need something to leverage myself back to life.'

'The trip . . .' she is staying with me.

'I'll finish the boat first, cabins for the girls, a new nav station, more bookshelves. I'd like to open up the main salon – a sort of family room – and add water tankage.'

'That's a year's work for a healthy person, John.'

'The guys will help me.'

'They probably will, but . . .'

'I feel better just *thinking* about it. I'll bet I can do it over the winter, be done by summer.'

Barbara looks at me evenly, a balancing act. I try to anticipate her reservations.

'We won't take the kids out there if I can't handle it. I just need something to reach for . . .'

Nothing.

Then Barbara shakes her head in practised bewilderment. She leans back and chuckles.

'You're crazier than a loon,' looking down, then back up. 'I love that about you.'

'That's a "yes"?'

More laughter, her whole body this time, her head thrown back.

•••••

FIRST OF ALL, I MUST SURVIVE, one deep breath at a time. Lying around all day is not my natural state. I try to read, a book propped awkwardly on my stomach. My eyes don't focus like before. All that anaesthesia? I close them in hopes of dozing off. I open them again, spend long periods studying the ceiling.

I know about heavy weather, I remind myself. *I have been here before*. I ride memory out beyond the bedroom walls, beyond my restlessness and distress. I am back on our first boat, *Outrageous*, six months into our first trip . . .

•••••

IT IS NOVEMBER IN 1989, on a seawall in Gibraltar. For eleven long days I have faced down Mary Kay's disappointment at having flown four thousand miles to languish in this smugglers' nest across the straits from Morocco. A longtime friend, she never openly complains. At the same time, a passage to the Canaries is what she's bargained for. Why did this series of monster lows pick November to park out there, directly in our path?

Be patient, I tell myself. We've got kids on board: John

Ryan is thirteen, Katie just shy of fourteen months. *If you have to go, you can't.*

At 9.30pm, friends on *Edgewater*, a gigantic motor yacht, bring us the news.

'The storm's moving on.'

Armed with an improving weather forecast, they are leaving, heading down the west coast of Africa for the Canaries. They are gone within the hour, disappearing into the darkness. We follow two hours later.

We pound out of the harbour and into the straits. It is rough going. A gusty Southwesterly is conspiring with two knots of tidal current to produce thoroughly confused seas.

Barbara soon retreats below to her bunk with Katie. John Ryan's attempts to settle her have uncharacteristically come up short. I shift back and forth at the helm, trying vainly to generate warmth. An hour out and I am already second-guessing our departure. It's not supposed to be like this.

I turn on our deck lights, attempting to make us visible to the thousand-tonne freighters who are making short work of the straits. They appear then disappear in the waves, in front of us and behind.

Miles ahead, the lights of Tangier reflect up on the boiling clouds. We just need to get across the straits and into the Atlantic. 'It should break by dawn.'

It doesn't.

Barbara takes the wheel just before daybreak. She guides us through the relative calm along the sheltering cliffs of Morocco. By the time I re-take the helm at 9am we are already fifteen miles out into the Atlantic. Far from clearing, however, the wind is still howling out of the South. We are probably on the edge of yet another countercyclical low.

'This was supposed to clear off.'

'So much for *suppose*.'

We furl our jib in another notch, and put another reef in the main. We push reluctantly to the Southwest. Even though we are angling directly into the storm, I want the space that deep water affords.

'Don't want to get pinned against that shore.'

We slog close-hauled into the blustery afternoon. Barbara pours out the hot chocolate and the stew, renewed warmth and energy in their wake.

'If we can punch through here,' I tell her, 'we should have Northwesterlies on the other side.' A sleigh ride to the Canaries, I hope.

It takes a while. The first wind shift comes in the early hours of the following morning. A stronger wind now, prompting a suggestion from Barbara that we put another reef in the mainsail. We decide to ride it out until daylight.

'It should weaken before then.'

First light arrives to a freight-train roar. I struggle out of my berth and up the companionway to the cockpit. Barbara smiles grimly at the helm. We scan the horizon in silence. The swells have flattened out under the sheer weight of the wind. *Outrageous* is flying.

'Better get that reef in,' she shouts. The mainsail doesn't wait for relief. Just as I get to the mast, the reef points give out, lines tearing vertically up into the sail. I slacken the flagging main, then struggle to put a reef in above the damage.

'It's going to tear out too!' Barbara warns.

She's probably right. Better to drop the main altogether.

Back in the cockpit, we hastily review our options. The Canaries are more than five hundred miles away. We are emotionally unwilling to retreat to Gibraltar, to face the winds that will inevitably shift to the North.

'Let's head South as much as we can, just ride it out. We can furl or unfurl the genny as we need.

'We'll play it *very* conservatively,' I add, hoping to reassure Barbara.

'Like always,' she looks away.

A quick consultation with the chart tells us that we are about seventy miles north of Casablanca.

'At the rate we are going, we might make it by dark. We can duck in there if we need to.'

'We don't have any charts for Casablanca,' Barbara counters.

I have no answer to the question in her voice.

Barbara relieves me in the early afternoon, piling on miles during a long downwind watch. *Outrageous* rockets down the swells at speeds over nine knots.

I pull myself back into the cockpit just before sunset. I am warm and dry again, fortified by a meal that Mary Kay has somehow pulled together. The kids continue to be resilient, high-spirited really, owing largely to John Ryan's capacity to dazzle his sister.

Life in the cockpit is a different matter. The winds are blowing a steady thirty-five under cloudless skies. The following growlers are enormous now, a steep twenty feet and angry. Our downwind speed bleeds off some of their power. I watch them wide-eyed, trying not to give in to fear. Barbara monitors my response, saying nothing. Then I look forward.

'Barbara, that's the shore out there.' A thin line of white water on the horizon, sandy coloured rock poking through the haze beyond.

'Just came into view,' she says, unhappy with my tone of voice.

Not good. We are pinned against a rocky coast. Pulling on my gloves, I glance over my shoulder at the horizon behind us, more closely this time.

'Damn. We've got a stormfront coming.'

Barbara twists around to squint at the black creeping up over the horizon.

'But we're already in a storm!'

'Let me take over,' I ask, more brusque than I intend. 'Please' – *stay calm* – 'get the chart from below.'

I experiment with the wheel, exploring our options. It is a relief to do something, to burn off fear with action. A foresail in this following wind won't work.

Barbara comes up the companionway with a planning chart. Casablanca is less than twenty miles away. We will have to turn into the wind to stay off the shore, almost directly into these huge swells. I turn on the engine, furl in what is left of our genny. We are able to hold our own, maybe even make some headway.

'Are you okay?' – and, when I nod – 'I need to get everyone squared away down below.' Barbara retreats down the companionway, pulling the hatch closed behind her. *Good luck.* She has the hardest job on board.

All hell breaks loose just after sunset. The lights on shore disappear first, lost in the frenzy that rolls over us. The bow lights disappear next.

'That's trouble,' I am talking to myself.

I push on glasses to protect my eyes from the suddenly horizontal spray. They are torn away immediately. My sense of direction is also stripped away, lost in the swirl of a wind which veers one way, then another.

I cannot see, cannot even look up. I hunch over the red glow of the compass, struggle to maintain a westerly heading. I try unsuccessfully to protect myself from the sleet-like onslaught. There is no discernible pattern to the swells, hammered down by the wind and rain, then surging up over us. No forgiveness. Pandemonium.

Just hang on. It can't last.

The storm cell moves through quickly. The bow lights blink back into view. The shore lights reappear minutes later. The storm hurls itself against the rocky hills beyond the shore. The wind drops back into the manageable thirties and begins a night-long shift towards the Northwest. I laugh out loud at the raw power of it, adrenaline and helplessness. I am drenched and frozen and wide awake.

Exhilaration gives way to awe when the big waves come. An Irish client of mine, a North Sea steward, once told me about them. I have seen a picture of them in a book, snapped from the bow of a freighter they were chasing. But these are not pictures of us now, and nothing in my experience has prepared me for them. I stand at the wheel and gape.

In less than an hour they grow to thirty feet. They pass through almost silently. In a few short hours they are forty feet high and vertical, up to the second spreaders on the mast. The biggest ones arrive in pairs, hiking up onto each other. They lift us effortlessly, the tiniest car at the amusement park. We are getting dropped now, down backsides so steep we free-fall into the trailing trough. *Outrageous* protests, shuddering each time we hit bottom. She cannot sustain this beating. She will come apart.

I am yanked to attention by the jarring. I instinctively angle off to starboard, ride the waveface up, and spin the wheel just as we crest. It works. We catch the backside of the wave with our beam, and rob our fall of its hull-caving velocity. The companionway hatch jolts open. Barbara thrusts her head out, overflowing with complaint. The sight of the next enormous wave silences her. I spin the wheel back to centre, and we begin our next breathless ascent. Our eyes lock in amazement, each crest a surprise. We begin to laugh. It is magic.

I can't hold her gaze. To miss even a single wave – the perfectly timed spin of the wheel – is to free-fall into the canyon behind, a boat-jarring shock. I quickly find a rhythm, a blurred cycle of awe at the approach, exhilaration at the lift, and the all-important swivel sideways at the crest.

The intensity is unsustainable. Barbara begins night-long ministrations of hot chocolate and cookies, Coke, crackers and candy bars to keep me going.

'It's beautiful,' she gasps after handing me a Coke. 'Takes your breath away.'

The swells begin to taper by first light, then drop off over time. We round the pierhead mid-morning and ride our last twenty-footer down behind the breakwater, into the uncanny calm of Casablanca's huge harbour system. Within an hour we motor into the small boat harbour in the oily backwaters. We tie up alongside a burly steel ketch.

Barbara helps me strip off my foul-weather gear. She checks on the sleeping children.

I collapse down onto a cockpit settee, warmed by the African sun. I am trembling with exhaustion, incapable of lifting an arm.

For a moment I am the happiest man alive . . .

•••••

MY CASABLANCA REVERIE IS BROKEN by the ringing phone, an acidy resentment at being dragged back into this day and place. I do not pick up the receiver, unwilling to respond to another well-intentioned inquisition about the sorry state of my health.

I'm sick, okay, and I may not get better!

Only later do I swallow my dread enough to remember that this is a storm also, storm of a different kind.

Is it possible to find the beauty in the mayhem?

•••••

SHORTLY AFTER LEAVING THE HOSPITAL, Barbara and I renew our weekly visits to my parents. I want to assure them that I am getting better. Their frail health distracts me from my own.

My 85-year-old father, deep in the throes of advanced Parkinson's, continues to give us a lesson in grace. Each encroaching month claims more of his resources, leaves him more isolated within the prison of his withering neurology. Thoughts are fleeting, as are the words to translate them. Getting out of a chair is an adventure, navigating the walk to the kitchen an uncertain voyage. The distance grows between plate and mouth, his lap full of scraps after a meal. Nothing is lost on this proud man, long set and solid in his dependable body. He shakes his head at the mess he is making, his frustration turning to humour as our eyes meet. *Deal with what is.*

Whatever the limits of his failing nervous system, he remains intact at another centre. His eyes brighten when we enter the room, his smile warmer even as the lights dim. What special wisdom informs him? Has he simply discovered the great gift that is being alive?

Tears often well before I reach the car, tears and a clenched jaw. I hate what the disease is doing to him. I am in awe of his unaffected capacity for joy, even as everything is being taken away.

He staggers out onto the side porch, waving to us as we pull away.

Can I live with his grace, wherever this goes?

• • • • •

SUMMER GIVES WAY TO AUTUMN, kids back to school, the first cold nights. I have been out of the hospital for a month now. My heart has still not exploded.

I take my first walk in September, two sunny blocks to a shop for a magazine. I slow to a crawl at the end of a block, and lie down in the grass to ease the ache in my chest. In time, my chest clears. I struggle to see the irony in this, the great runner at the end of the day. I straggle back home later, chastened for my illusions.

Within weeks I am walking further, hoping the pain of exertion will spur the growth of new collateral arteries. A threshold is crossed when I first take Shiva with me. An energetic chocolate lab, she tugs me along with a squall's insistence, ever eager for the mysteries of the next garden. I remind her I am an invalid, but it doesn't slow her pace. *Invalid, schminvalid* her yellow eyes seem to say.

I begin seeing clients again; an hour at first, then two. Some are alarmed by my calmness. *Are you going to die?* I see it another way – more to do with health. Slower feels better now, sometimes almost natural.

I pull myself away from college football for a Saturday in early October to brainstorm with Dan, Barry and David about the next generation of upgrades for *Grace*. They are familiar with the longstanding routine: I'll roll out some extravagant project and try to rope them into it.

'That sounds terrific, John. But what does this have to do with *us?*' deadpans David.

'Seems like a big job for a guy to do alone,' Dan adds without a trace of irony.

'You're pretty good at dreaming this stuff up,' Barry is shaking his head. 'I can hardly keep up with your fantasy life.'

They sign up with their disdain. 'Here we go again!'

Our friends' generosity is not to be confused with enthusiasm for our proposed trip. Some think we are deranged even to consider it. Any mention of 'the trip' these days is most often met with a telling silence. On one occasion, Barry confronts me directly: 'I think you're being irresponsible, John, to even think about taking Barbara and the girls to sea, with your heart.'

We clear the air somewhat during a long dinner discussion. Barbara sheds any impression that she's being dragged into a suicide mission.

'Did it ever occur to you that being away from the pressure of work – spending all day, every day, in beautiful places with our girls – might actually be a pretty healthy thing to do?'

A truce of sorts is reached, an informal agreement to disagree. The same Barry who challenges me most directly also volunteers long weekends renovating *Grace*.

• • • • •

BY THE END OF OCTOBER I am walking several miles every morning, slowing my pace somewhat when the pain exceeds '5' on a 1 to 10 scale. I can feel my heart start to malfunction dangerously at about '7'. The secret is to push myself hard enough to sustain a tolerable level of pain, pain that argues chemically for the growth of new collaterals. I am banking on the heart's wisdom, on its innate instinct to protect itself and survive. The strategy raises some eyebrows among my physician friends. Not enough to slow my pace.

Exercise is only a small part of reordering my life. *What counts?* Although I pay lip service to the value of both action and contemplation, I log more time on the action side of the ledger. It's time to restore some balance.

Health is understandably in the spotlight now, a renewed commitment to diet and rest. Resting is the hard part. Slowing my pace requires attention. I remind myself over and over to do less, more consciously and contentedly.

Time with the kids moves to a position of primacy. I don't know how long I have to live. I do know they will be out of the door before long. John Ryan's sudden eruption into adulthood reminds Barbara and me how little time we have. I don't want to miss any of it.

Barbara and I have long made our relationship a priority, buttressed with weekly dates. Time together – dinner, the bookshop, or a movie – helps sustain a romance we need now more than ever.

The abrupt immersion in mortality also deepens my hunger to live wide awake, a staple in my spirituality. Life is a gift. I don't want to sleepwalk through it, or rush through it on automatic pilot. I want to be conscious of every moment: to fully register the magic a falling leaf imparts on October; the sadness in the cashier's eyes. To really hear Erin singing herself to sleep.

The ache in my chest is a wake-up call.

I want the same intense involvement in life that the poet describes, the relationship a man whose hair is on fire has with an icy pond. My life is on fire. I will not survive. I want to be fully alive, for as long as I can.

•••••

'THE TRIP' SEEMS TO EMBODY many of the priorities Barbara and I share at this stage of our lives: a decompression from professional work; twenty-four-hour days with each other and the girls; the challenge and mystery of the wilderness sea; the slower pace that invites full attention.

Barbara, beneficiary of an educator's gene, is excited about 'boat schooling' the girls. 'It'll be a pain sometimes, but I'm looking forward to it.'

I plan to write. I have dreamed about it since adolescence. The ease of fantasy, without the discipline or risk.

'I'll have time, finally. No excuses.'

I plan to use the girls' school hours to take out my words at last. A wiser person might be reluctant to start something new this late in life, raw and untrained. I am energized by the knowledge that I will never catch up.

'Imagine hearing Beethoven for the first time at fifty-five.'

Barbara rolls her eyes and groans.

•••••

NOVEMBER ARRIVES TIMIDLY, then accelerates with each deepening Northwesterly. *Grace*, cheated by my faulty heart of a full-bore summer, now sits forlornly on a cradle for the winter.

David and I climb up a ladder to her deck. My chest throbs from the exertion and the cold. I slip a nitro under my tongue before untying the ropes on the boat cover. We slither under it and into the cockpit. I remove the companionway slats and step down into the cabin. The electric heaters will take some time to cut into the chill. We sit in their red glow, bundled up, breath steaming.

I explain my plans one more time.

'I won't be much good with the woodwork, John. I can help with the plumbing and electrics.'

'That'd be terrific, Davey.'

'I've already pencilled in lines for cutting away these two bulkheads,' I continue.

David leans in and squints at the faint pencil marks. They extend from cabin sole to cabin top, then six feet down a centreline bulkhead. A second set of lines outlines a four-foot section, from the centreline across to the hull.

'If you've got the time, I'd like to cut them right now.'

David doesn't respond immediately, staring sceptically

at the endangered bulkheads. I reach for a circular saw and plug it in.

'I don't know, John,' turning towards me. 'Are you sure?'

'Of course not. But it's time to get started.'

I put the heel of the saw up against the bulkhead, sighting in the line beneath the blade. I glance at David, looking for affirmation. He is examining his boots, muttering. *Here we go again.*

I look back to the bulkhead, sight in again. The saw screams to attention. I ease its blade down into the line. A shower of enamel-laced sawdust explodes from beneath it, filling the cabin.

Half an hour later, I drop the saw, now burning my hands, onto a cushionless settee. I collapse down beside it, wet with exertion, plastered with sawdust, an ache in my chest. David is perched stoically across from the severed bulkheads, his hat and shoulders tan with dust.

'Well, you've done it now, John,' the beginning of a grin.

'. . . Again,' he adds emphatically.

I smile through the sawdust-caked surface of my face, for just a moment out beyond uncertainty and hesitation.

'No turning back now.'

•••••

I AM NOT FEELING GOOD YET. I am feeling better. Daily work-outs usher me into the wilderness of pain, although it does take longer to reach the point where my heart seriously misfires. When it does, I back off quickly. No more heart attacks.

It has been almost four months since I've been in the hospital. Today I go back, to find out if the exercise has done any good. A Thallium stress test will map with radio-active precision the flow of blood to my heart, during physical stress and rest.

The technician inserts the needle with uncommon efficiency. She shaves my chest, and tapes the electrodes in place. I sprawl beneath the arching arm of the x-ray machine.

'Stay perfectly still.'

The isotopes are injected, a cool procession up my arm. The twenty-minute procedure of picture-taking begins, a weighty click at regular intervals. A second injection is made minutes into a treadmill work-out, an ominous level '7' ache in my chest. Another set of x-rays and scans follow exercise. I shiver in the cold.

Rick pores over the results later, mixing questions with feedback. While the blood supply is clearly deficient in the area supplied by the LAD, my heart can now sustain moderate stress before it lurches in the direction of a full-blown attack. There is definite improvement from August's low point.

'Those collateral arteries are picking up some of the slack,' Rick seems relieved. 'Keeping you alive. Whatever you're doing is working.'

'I'm pushing myself, Rick. If I'm going to have problems, I'd rather have them before we leave.'

'Still thinking about the trip?' he asks, as casually as possible.

'We want to go if we can.'

'When?'

'Next summer – June or July.'

'I'm not sure we're going to know enough by then,' he offers tentatively.

'If we go, we'll spend at least six months sailing down the East Coast,' Barbara chimes in.

'Probably no ocean crossing for at least eight months,' I add.

'Well, that gives us a little more of a safety net,' Rick tries. 'The safest thing, of course, would be to stay put.'

'I don't want to be glib, Rick' – *take a breath* – 'but there's a lot more to safety than being a few minutes from the hospital.'

Rick nods stoically.

After an awkward silence, I try to reassure him, without giving ground.

'We won't leave at all if we think it is going to put us or the girls at risk,' as much for Barbara as for him. 'But we're in the grey zone here. And I'm not convinced that giving up the trip – at this point – will help.'

Rick says nothing for a moment, then replies evenly, 'I'm not either.'

In the car, I sound out Barbara. 'You okay with what I said in there?'

'Yes, I am.' Then, just a hint of a smile, 'How do you *really* feel, John?'

She is laughing now.

•••••

WINTER DEEPENS AS JANUARY DRONES TO A CLOSE. It is dark when we rise and dark when we leave the office in the evening. The brain hungers for the chemical lift of sunlight.

'I won't miss this part,' Barbara gestures out of the windshield, dismissing the smothering gloom.

The passage of time has a different feel for us this season. Each day, each week, is another step away from hospitalization. It has been five months since they last laid me down, filled me full of needles, cut on me. We have been holding our breath for a year, always aware that the other shoe could drop any time.

We are starting to exhale.

I live with an ache in my chest, but it is the ache of an unexploded heart. Even the numbers are starting to work for us. The actuarial charts I scrutinize at the medical library indicate that most re-stenosis occurs within six months. Can I see the light?

After a long discussion with Barbara, I shift my practice schedule in the direction of the trip. I will now see clients only four days a week, leaving three to work on the boat. It is a perfect blend, I rationalize: two days of therapeutic intensity followed by a knuckle-busting day with the saw and the drill and the sander.

Grace needs all the time I can give her. I have once again bitten off more than I can chew, even with the generosity of Dan, David and Barry. One of them – most often Dan – works with me many weekends. During the week I work alone. It is work I have come to enjoy, perhaps the long shadow of ancestors.

I can hear the clock running in the background, six months and counting.

I try to save the heavy lifting for days when I have help. Sometimes it can't wait. On one occasion, I am blown off the ladder when a wintry gust catches the sail area of a four-by-eight-foot section of marine plywood. I let go of the plywood midair, trying to break my fall. It lands on top of me after I hit the ground.

The snow cushions my fall. Everything is shockingly still, flakes settling on my jacket and jeans. I am okay, other than the weight in my chest. I fish for a nitro, amazed at my good luck. Nothing broken, nothing lost.

Later, in the relative warmth of the cabin, the energy goes out of me. It is only 11.30am, and I am already exhausted, exasperated at finding that one of the three water tanks I am installing will not fit under a settee.

My mind is racing with the seemingly endless 'things to do' list that woke me at 4am. Momentarily overwhelmed, I struggle to remember the pay off in going to sea.

I reach up and turn off the overhead lights. The boat's interior is outlined in the faint glow of the electric heaters. The wind howls outside, clawing at the canvas boat cover. I roll a sweatshirt into a makeshift pillow, and stretch out on the cushionless settee.

Memory takes over, gobbling up the time I intend for sleep. I drift back to our first trip, to John Ryan's passage within a passage . . .

· · · · ·

JOHN RYAN AND I SET SAIL FROM SAINT THOMAS to New York in the April of 1990. He has recently turned fourteen. It is the last offshore leg of our first, sixteen-month family cruise. Barbara responds to his insistent 'you and I ought to sail to New York alone' by pulling me aside and – to my surprise – agreeing.

'I think you ought to take him up on it. Just the two

of you, a father–son adventure. Katie and I can fly to New York, hang out with your cousin, David. Be waiting for you.'

When I say nothing, she adds, 'It may be a long time before the two of you get another chance to do something like this.' John's burgeoning adolescence isn't lost on either of us.

I am intrigued, only later relent.

We leave in the late afternoon. Barbara holds Katie at the end of the dock, waving.

She knows this is a voyage infused with meaning: a week or two at sea, alone with our son, the boy in transit.

We stop to fuel up, then make our way out of the harbour and around the western tip of Saint Thomas, out into open water. The shore lights eventually disappear in the dark.

The next week takes us, on fair winds mostly, around Puerto Rico, past the Dominican Republic and the Bahamas, and up the Eastern Seaboard. Two days south of Cape Hatteras, the wind shifts to the Southwest, stabilizes, then intensifies. For the next thirty-six hours we rocket along, impervious to the growing swells. The wind shifts again, this time to the Northwest.

An afternoon racket signals a broken main halyard. While I am puzzling over the frazzled wires shackled to the head of the deflated sail, John struggles to unfasten our second halyard from the toerail. I move to help him, but too late. The shackle gets away from him and flies wildly out over the waves. We grab at it helplessly as the halyard works its way up towards the top of the mast.

'I'm sorry, Dad.'

'It's done,' an unnatural calm. 'Let go of it.'

'I already did,' he shoots back, smiling sheepishly.

We are 140 miles from Norfolk now, and 380 from New York. We have no halyards with which to hoist our mainsail. We do have a taut foresail, and a buffeting wind that wants to take us further out into the Atlantic, away from Norfolk or New York.

We also have several hours of daylight.

We head downwind, to steady *Outrageous* as much as possible. John then attempts to hoist me to the top of the mast on a spinnaker halyard. It doesn't work. He doesn't yet have the bulk to heft me up, not on a pitching deck.

'Let me try, Dad. You crank me up.'

I am hesitant to do it. He is strong but scrawny, eager but untested.

'Are you sure? It will be a rough ride. You're going to have to hang on.'

'I think I can do it, Dad.' Then, taking the bosun's chair out of my hands, 'Let me try.'

I secure the chair with the other spinnaker halyard. Repeating a mistake I made earlier, I do not tether him to the mast.

'Are you sure?' I ask as he is settling in.

'Not entirely,' he smiles. 'Let's try it.'

I winch him up a little at a time. He clings to the mast like a frightened monkey, G-forces increasing as he goes higher. A particularly brutish wave throws us just as he is pulling himself onto the first spreader. He momentarily loses his grip and catapults out over the side, grabbing a shroud as he swings by.

For a second he is caught midstream, stretched out

horizontally between the bosun's chair he is sitting in and the shroud he is clinging to. Then the boat rocks back, slamming him against the shroud.

'Dad, get me down!'

Back on the deck, he is thoroughly shaken, the deep rose of a bruise spreading out across his hip.

'Good job, good job,' I keep repeating in relief, an arm around his shoulder.

'I didn't do anything.'

'You hung on.' I lead him back to the cockpit.

After a hot bowl of soup, we can laugh about it.

'Thrills and spills,' he enthuses.

There are few things I miss about adolescence. From a distance of decades it mostly resembles a series of accidents. If you're lucky, you live for another day, the beguiling possibility of yet another accident.

But I do admire the sheer resiliency of the survivors, the speed with which they heal, their unfounded willingness to hurtle back into the arena. So I shouldn't be surprised at John's response to my decision to shimmy up the mast.

'No, you won't,' he announces with a steely determination.

'I did it coming across,' I counter.

'Please, Dad,' softening now. 'Let me try again.'

'It's too risky.'

'Not as risky as your trying to shimmy up it,' with an authority he rarely exhibits in peacetime.

When I pause, he bores in: 'I *need* to do this. And I *can.*'

His mouth is set, granite in his jaw.

'Please let me try. I'll come down if I can't handle it.'

There are moments in every relationship when the weight shifts perceptibly. In the vacuum between instants, a new centre of gravity is established. We balance mid-air, looking straight into each other. I finally nod a wordless assent. He waits, as if for the shift to register, then nods back.

'Thanks, Dad.'

Back on the open deck, I second-guess myself. The mast is flailing around.

'Are you sure?' as he picks up the bosun's chair.

'Yes, I am.' A resolve that startles.

I look up the mast. The shackle is still there, shifting with each pitch and roll.

I look back, one last check in his eyes. He does not flinch, not even a flutter.

'Hoist me up, Captain.'

'You hang on, hotshot,' and give him a pat on the cheek. 'And put this safety tether around the mast.'

'Aye, aye,' he shoots back with reassuring insolence.

It's hard to develop any rhythm with the winch while keeping an eye on him. Up past the first spreader he encounters serious G-forces, the waves' attempt to catapult him out to sea. He detaches the tether, reattaching it above the spreader. He bangs around, but holds on. As he ascends, his legs join his arms in an embrace of the pirouetting mast. At the second spreader, he repeats the procedure, flailing for several long seconds on one side of the mast, then the other. I furiously crank him high enough so he can rewrap his legs, reattach the tether.

'You okay?' I shout up into the wind.

'Take me on up.'

I crank as steadily as possible.

'Stop there,' he barks down.

I tie him off and reach for the binoculars. One arm around a shroud, I focus in with the other hand. John and the mast vault back and forth, either side of my magnified vision. I finally zero in just as he pulls the halyard out with his left hand, arm fully extended, holding on with the other.

But these are not the arms of a boy, the flared muscles and powerful hands. It is not a boy's neck that bulges from beneath the blowing mane, nor a boy's legs locked around the mast.

'Lower me slowly.'

The sound cascades down. It is the voice of a man.

• • • • •

I'M NOT READY TO RELINQUISH THE WARMTH of memory. I'm not eager to go out in the cold and re-tie the ladder that is rattling against the toerail. And I'm in no rush to face the incorrigible water tank.

I groan and roll over – *get moving* – and pull myself up off the settee. I have not fallen asleep. I am energized by a son I am proud of, the pure fuel of realized dreams.

Tomorrow's dreams want today's pound of flesh. This morning – *that damn water tank* – some imagination and grit.

• • • • •

IF I AM WORKING HARD, it is Barbara who shoulders most of the load. Ever since my open-heart surgery, she has taken over morning duty. While I doze back off for an hour or so, she rousts the kids out, oversees their washing and breakfast, and carts them off to school.

Taking the pressure off me is her way of dealing with the uncertainty that dogs us. She rarely complains, although she does let the veil drop long enough to tell a friend, 'I now know what it must be like to live with cancer. It can come back any minute. There's nothing we can do about it.'

Barbara's sense of powerlessness deepens as I extend my work schedule – at the office or boat – further into the evening. Her exasperation about my momentum-gathering pace spills over in minutes of weariness.

'I'm doing everything I can to reduce the wear and tear on you. And you just keep piling it on.'

When I don't respond, she keeps coming.

'It's only been six months since you were at death's door. You are now sleeping an extra hour – if you call it sleeping – and working seven days a week!'

'The boat work is relaxing' – *I've got to head this off* – 'a welcome break from therapy.'

'And you're up at three in the morning, adding to your "things to do" list,' she spits. 'Tell me about *relaxing*.'

'It's also entertaining' – *maybe humour will work* – 'because I don't know what I'm doing.'

Barbara's not buying into playfulness tonight.

'Try to see it my way, John. I'm scared to death. I work my butt off to protect you, and I watch you drag yourself home, dead tired, at ten at night. I'm afraid you're going to have another heart attack.'

In case that didn't take, 'I'm afraid you're going to *die!*'

No glib evasion this time. Her concerns run deep, and

I don't want to add to them. Nor do I have any interest in dying.

'I'm not trying to beat you up,' she says, more softly now that she has my full attention.

'I know you aren't. And I *am* trying to pace myself – to get the job done *and* take care of myself. It's a balancing act. Everything takes three times as long as I thought. Not a right angle inside that hull. I have to draw templates for every piece of wood I cut, then cut it again.'

She doesn't once say 'I told you so,' although we both know she could. *I love this woman.*

'I do think the physical work is helping my heart. I am sleeping a little better.' *Don't take advantage of the room she has given.*

'I know I can get too tired, and set myself up for problems. But I've got to get *Grace* finished before we can move onto her and leave.'

Barbara shifts in her seat. She is running out of patience.

'Maybe we ought to push back our departure date . . .'

My heart sinks: flashes of a year-long delay.

'. . . Shoot for the beginning of August rather than the end of May,' she continues. 'Take a little pressure off you, give ourselves an extra two months to pay for the upgrades.'

Even with reduced wattage, I know a good deal when I see one.

'That would give us more time to see how my heart is working, a little more breathing room . . .'

'Can we leave in August and get through the Great Lakes to the Atlantic, before the Northerlies kick in?' Barbara defers to me where geography is involved.

'We can probably make it without breaking our necks.'

When she says nothing, I seal the deal. 'I think it makes sense.'

We both exhale a bit, wrapping ourselves in the illusion that an extra sixty days will actually reduce the wear and tear.

• • • • •

THERE IS MORE TO LEAVING THAN JUST GETTING *Grace* ready. The most important preparation has skin on.

The kids are resilient, but continue to struggle with the uncertainty of it all. They go for months without knowing, on any given night, whether we will be at home or at the hospital when they awake. Or whether I am coming home at all.

Of the three, nine-year-old Katie seems the most adversely affected, traumatized by the mid-August retreat from *Grace* to the hospital, being passed to friends when I am rushed through the emergency room doors. In spite of our efforts to reassure her, she is haunted and distracted at school, her natural aptitude cloaked in anxieties we cannot sweep away. Her studies suffer as we straggle through winter, her late-blooming reading abilities exacerbated by concerns about me.

Katie's fears mirror our own, however we try to live out beyond them. We try to normalize her life and ours, and seek outside help for her reading. We spend long hours with her, equal parts ventilation and reassurance. How to free her from fears we share? Every month without hospitalization helps.

Five-year-old Erin rallies more easily, as does her older brother, John. She is well served by an attention span short enough that she doesn't stray far from the here and now. She seems to ride an inborn exuberance through good days and difficult, greeting each morning with an irrepressible buoyancy.

John Ryan, no stranger to turmoil as a teenager, draws on a strength and calm not in evidence during those years. He runs on his own fuel now, lurching good naturedly from one adventure to the next. Having weathered the hurricane of emancipation, he stands comfortably on his own. Barbara and I make peace with his staying in Michigan. He has a job now, a girlfriend, and college to finish. He seems energized by his newfound independence.

'It's time to build a life, Dad. My own life.'

I am buttressed by a good relationship with my parents. My dad and I have been solid for a long time, mostly able to celebrate our many differences. I am in awe of his grace and certainty, even as Parkinson's undermines his neurology. He seems entertained by my more quixotic take on life. We regularly look at each other and laugh, shaking our heads in mirror image.

My relationship with my mother is more complicated. Contentment comes in smaller snatches for her. Irish agitation is her natural state, perhaps her way of fending off the indignities of aging, hostage now of a bone structure as fragile as porcelain. For as long as I can remember, from those earliest intimations of my ranginess, we have jousted over the same issues, almost a dance.

'Johnny, when are you going to settle down?'

'I've taken a good look at "settled down", Mom. It's not all it's cracked up to be.'

At this point, she summons her considerable indignation, and shudders graphically, her shoulders pressed up
for emphasis.

In recent years, our intransigence clearly established,
we adapt a short form of the ritual, one where she simply
asks about my timetable for 'settling down'. She pauses
long enough for our eyes to register, then breaks into
laughter.

I like this version better. A cryptic code for recogni-
tion that we are different, and perhaps an unsteady acceptance.

'Don't get too carried away,' my sister would say.

While I am at peace with my parents, I am tormented
by their physical decline, and the knowledge that I will not
be there for them.

My brother Jim and I take a springtime walk together,
through the neighbourhood we roamed as boys. We
compare notes about the old days and now, going over it
again.

'I really want to go: step back from all this for a while,
spend the time with Barbara and the girls.'

'Then you should,' he cuts in, intercepting the concerns
I have raised about his shouldering the weight of our
parents' care.

'Don't get me wrong – Diane and I both think you're
crazy. Heart or no heart, I don't for a second "get it". But
I know you. You've got this cockeyed dream. You'd be a
damn fool not to do it.

'We'll take care of the folks,' he continues. 'Hell, I'm
not going anywhere, and I'd rather walk on glass than go
out there.'

The same absolutist edge I often tease him about is comforting in this context. Gruff love. He would gag if I pointed it out. Jim has scant tolerance for anything he perceives as complimentary, or worse yet, sentimental.

We walk on.

'I know that you're doing this for your own reasons, Jim.' *Keep it short.* 'Your taking over makes the trip possible. Thank you for that.'

For a change, he doesn't backhand me.

My parents and sister are as supportive as they can be. They understand taking time off to spend with our girls, particularly in light of my precarious health. Sailing across oceans leaves them cold, a nondescript blankness flooding their faces. Sometimes a dismissive shaking of heads.

This is a dance we all know well, parts scripted over half a century together. Our parents' frailty magnifies everything. Although I will find it difficult to be away, I take comfort in the perhaps rationalized sense that we are all playing out longstanding roles. I am moved by their reticent but real capacity to support me.

•••••

BARBARA'S FAMILY PRESENTS A SIMPLER, but more painful set of circumstances. Her mother, a casualty of advanced Alzheimer's, has been receiving nursing home care for seven years. Her inability to recognize anyone often leaves Barbara sobbing in the car after visits. She has left us long before her death.

Barbara's father, a veteran of the cardiac wars himself, is an energized seventy-five. He is sad yet supportive of his

daughter's leaving, and eager to use our trip as an excuse
to travel more than he already does.

Barbara's sister, Audrey, an avid traveller herself, will
miss the proximity of her best friend. She promises to visit
us regularly with her husband, Russ, and son, Ben.

For our part, we determine that I will attempt to visit
my parents every three or four months, accompanied by
Barbara and the girls when we can afford it. We will make
an extended pilgrimage home for Christmas each year,
regardless of price.

•••••

OUR FRIENDS CONTINUE TO RESPOND with predictable
diversity to the prospect of our leaving. The major concern
is that I might be stricken at sea. No talk of equipment or
precaution does much to extinguish this.

I want to think that my heart is improving, to dispel
the uncertainty with which we all uncomfortably co-exist.
It is hard not to get discouraged on days when the ache is
worse. I remind myself that progress must be measured in
months.

Pain is the bottom line. My heart does not complain
when it is getting enough blood. When overextension, cold
or runaway emotions cut into its chronically limited flow,
the heart muscles let me know with a deepening ache. *Give
us some help here, or there will be hell to pay.*

Daily workouts on the Stairmaster always usher me
down into pain. I try to push hard, but not so hard that I
have another heart attack. It would be easier if I was better
at moderation.

Discussions with Barbara prepare both of us for talking

with others. She regularly quizzes me about the status of my heart. I can only tell her how I feel. We speculate about what it means. Does seven months without a major episode signal an end to the deterioration? The bald truth is that nobody, not Rick, not his army of assistants with their machines, not the experts he is in contact with around the country, not one of them can know with any degree of certainty what's going on in these remaining two arteries.

'If they stop falling apart,' I tell Barbara, 'I could live thirty years. Not just survive, *live*.'

Rick serves up encouragement whenever we get together.

'Whatever you're doing seems to be working. I don't have to understand it to like it. Keep it up. A lot of us are watching.'

• • • • •

GRACE IS SCHEDULED TO BE LAUNCHED at Whitehall during the last week of April.

Barbara and I rearrange our schedules in order to be there when the hoist eases *Grace* down into the water.

'It's another day at work for these guys,' I tell her. 'Feels like a victory to me.'

Grace is the only boat in the water, bobbing alongside the seawall at the Crosswinds Marina. We fire her up for a two-minute trip to the slip where we will finish the renovations.

Two minutes is more than enough to flirt with disaster.

'Sure is blowing a lot of smoke,' I point out to Dale, the marina mechanic who fixes my mistakes.

'Let's take a look.'

We clear away the debris on the cabin sole, and remove the floor panels over the engine. Dale leans in, working his way quickly through a checklist he keeps in his head. He finally twists off the oil cap.

'Damn, John, there's water in the oil!'

'That's not good.' *Did I screw up again?*

'That's *really* bad,' something I've never heard him say before.

I resort to deep breathing as he makes his way around the engine. I try unsuccessfully not to jump to dire conclusions. *Where will we find the money for an engine rebuild?*

'Hey, John, where's the hose to the anti-siphon valve?'

It's hard, even if you're Irish, to answer questions posed in a foreign tongue.

'Well . . . what do you mean, Dale?'

Within minutes he locates the problem. When I took out the offending centre bulkhead, I coiled the anti-siphon extension into an adjacent locker, intending to work it into a new location later. *Later* got away from me. Water has flowed back through the exhaust system, directly into the engine.

'How bad is it?'

'The engine wasn't on for long, and it's not salt water. I'll have to go in there, get the water out, and take a look.' It sounds like Rick describing an angiogram.

Dale notices the anguish on my face. 'John, you're the luckiest person I know.'

'It'd be nice if I had a little expertise to go with it.'

● ● ● ● ●

DALE HAS ALREADY BEEN TO WORK when I clamber down the companionway a day later. There is greasy evidence everywhere. I walk up to the office in search of him, steeling myself against his diagnosis. He is in the tool shop, grinding away at a freshly welded pipe.

He turns off the grinder, pushes up his protective mask, and answers the question I am about to ask.

'I'd rather be lucky than smart.'

• • • • •

WE RENDEZVOUS AT RICK'S OFFICE in Grand Rapids towards the end of May. Barbara and I make our closing arguments for going to sea. When we finish, Rick stares down at the hands in his lap, looking for the right words. After a long time, and in a very measured tone, he counters.

'I have to tell you, John, I'm not crazy about your going out there.'

He pauses again, perhaps remembering that it has been only nine months since our heart transplant discussion.

'Then again, I have no way of explaining how you've come this far.'

'Maybe dreams have something to do with it, Rick.' Just in case he didn't get it the first time, 'Maybe *this* dream.'

Barbara's eyes brighten, but she says nothing.

Rick has done his job, but he's outnumbered here. His stern facade gives way.

'Okay, okay! I know when I can't win. But you get in here for regular check-ups.'

'Every time I come home.'

'Now, what can I do to help?'

•••••

Instead of going directly to the car after our appointment, I lead Barbara over to the lawn outside Rick's office. We sprawl in the grass, warmed by the late-spring sun. It is an uncommon pause for either of us these days.

We are quiet for a while. I swat away a persistent fly.

Finally, in a voice struggling to be nonchalant, Barbara asks, 'So what do you think?'

'I think we should go for it.'

She rolls onto her side, looks me straight in the eye, and nods. 'So do I.'

•••••

I adjust my work schedule another notch in the direction of leaving. I now see clients three days a week, working the other four days on *Grace*. The days are sprinting by now, the afternoons almost balmy, the smell of freshly mown grass. The sun holds on later each day, pushing evening back.

I need all the daylight I can get. I have seriously underestimated the work to do. As June closes in, the end is nowhere in sight. People who stop by are unable to disguise their alarm. The girls' rooms are half-built, the wiring and plumbing still exposed.

'No way,' one mutters as they climb off the boat and move down the dock. 'He'll never get it done in time.'

They are half-right. There is no way I will get *Grace* ready alone. But Dan Hendrickson has come aboard, carpentry skills and generosity in equal portions. Dan alone never questions the wisdom of the trip, telling others it is a good idea, if a bit gamey. He does better than talk, spending hours, then days, then whole weekends helping me work bulkheads and lockers and berths into the curved confines of the hull. He takes on the teak trim that must be painstakingly cut, sanded and varnished, bringing to the project a finesse I don't possess.

'Just bring along your sense of humour,' he reminds me.

When crunch-time arrives, Dan gives up midweek days of professional work to bust his knuckles alongside me.

Katie comes up on us one afternoon while we are struggling with an unwieldy bulkhead. She shouts her encouragement: 'You can do it, Dad. You're the man of steel.'

Grinning up at Dan, she adds '. . . and you're his trusty sidekick.'

We laugh, Dan loudest of all. Katie wanders down the dock, looking for just the right place to drop a fishing line over the side. When she is out of earshot, Dan shoots me a sideways glance, eyes full of mischief.

'How about *tin man?*' I try to cut him off.

'Better . . .' he smiles, never pausing in his effort to bury a screw.

• • • • •

IN 1981, WE MOVED INTO AN OLD DUTCH COLONIAL HOUSE, deep in an inner-city neighbourhood in Grand Rapids. We love it there, still live there today. When we first moved in, the neighbourhood was populated with the urban poor, renting mostly, from landlords who lived in the suburbs. Once people got to know you, and got beyond the suspicion that you might equate your whiteness with superiority, you were at least occasionally welcomed into an unembarrassed running dialogue about the quirkiness of poverty. A standing joke involved the apocryphal owner of a big, shiny, less than new, eight-cylinder Buick, standing in proud contrast before a ramshackle house:

'I can live in my car.

'I can't drive my house.'

Grace is a nautical offshoot of the neighbourhood parable. The renovations down below will make her family-friendly. She should be capable of taking us anywhere in the world. We can anchor where we want and move when we are ready. And, like the Buick down the street, we can live in her too.

I keep this in mind on days when dark doesn't arrive soon enough, when the ache comes to get me.

While I rush to get *Grace* ready for an August departure, Barbara takes charge of the enormous shore campaign. She and the children sort through our belongings, the largest pile to be sold or given to charity. John Ryan, who has recently moved into his own house, has right of first refusal on everything but the small portion we will pack away. We must pare our possessions by 90%. Only the absolutely essential make the final cut, the few boxes marked '*Grace*.'

More than a tepid gesture in the direction of simplification, this feels life-altering. The process of letting go of prized possessions is especially hard for Katie and Erin. Barbara and I lather on healthy portions of empathy and encouragement, discussing the value of experience over 'stuff'. Perhaps it will be obvious later. Perhaps for us also.

Barbara also shoulders the job of finding tenants for

our house. This is no easy task. During the almost twenty years we have lived here, the neighbourhood has edged slowly in the direction of gentrification. Urban pioneers are rediscovering the unique possibility embedded in older, rundown, irreplaceable homes.

'Those rich folks are moving in and wrecking the neighbourhood,' the locals say.

But we are early in the process, and most people are still leery about the area. Renting our house will be a challenge. Knowing that we will depend on the rent for our groceries ups the ante considerably. It is pressure neither of us needs.

Clearing out rooms also brings some unneeded surprises.

'There's plaster to be patched behind Katie's bed.'

'We'll have to paint that ceiling in the pantry.'

It is hard not to feel overwhelmed by all there is to be done.

When my resolve falters, I draw energy from an experience on our first trip. It is the spring of 1990 again, in Antigua . . .

•••••

WE HAD ANCHORED IN ENGLISH HARBOUR the evening before, worn out by the thrashing we took on our passage from Guadalupe. After sleeping late into the next day, we blow up the dinghy and go ashore, swimming suits and water toys on an almost empty beach. Barbara and I are stunned by the daytime beauty of the place, the white sand highlighting the deep turquoise of the water. Palm trees border the beach, and beyond them lush undergrowth drapes the encircling hills. A steel drum band is warming up at a nearby veranda bar, the music drifting out on an offshore breeze.

'Incredible,' Barbara stops spreading out the beach towels long enough to take it all in.

'Wouldn't you like to beam in our friends?'

Katie, six months afoot, is waddling around the beach, searching for anything she might stick in her mouth before we can stop her. Old cigarette butts are a favourite.

John Ryan, always pent-up after a passage, coaxes me into a football session.

'I'll do all the running, Dad.'

Later, I make my way up to the bar to get us a couple of beers. A tanned thirty-year-old notices me when I walk in, wrenching his attention away from the bikinied woman sitting next to him. He pushes his Raybans back and nods out at the harbour.

'Nice boat.'

'Thank you. We like her.'

He swivels playfully back to his companion. 'And I bet they're not paying $475 a night.'

'Are you kidding me?' I must be thoroughly out of touch with the going rates.

'Four hundred and seventy-five big ones a night for our bungalow.' He draws out the $475.

'We ought to get a sailboat,' he is back to her. 'Save a lot of money . . .'

Back on the beach, I tell the story to Barbara. 'Four hundred and seventy-five dollars . . . And us, out on the anchor, for free.'

'Not bad,' she smiles.

I sprawl back on my elbows, working my heels down into the sand. It's not so much a bargain as a trade-off. We are paying with the portfolio we are not amassing for time with our kids and each other. The wealth of needing less.

'And they'll be climbing back on a plane next week.'

•••••

JERRY BEURKENS, AN ATTORNEY FRIEND, catches up with me outside the health club at the Amway Grand Plaza Hotel in Grand Rapids.

'So you're really going to do it?'

'Going to give it a go, Jer.'

Jerry's momentary silence takes me by surprise. He never shuts up, his life a long, good-natured monologue. Finally he looks up from a thoughtful inspection of the ground.

'I don't know how to say this, John . . .'

'Fancy that.' We both grin.

'A lot of us admire what you're doing, envy you really . . .' he hesitates, '. . . but we worry about what could happen out there.'

'What do you have in mind?'

'I just hope you don't die,' he blurts, then reddens at his forthrightness.

We stand awkwardly for a second, lost for words.

'I appreciate your concern, Jerry.' I give him a playful hug, then step back.

'I'm going out there to *live*.'

•••••

BARBARA IS EXAMINING THE CALENDAR, plotting a Father's Day get-together for mid-June.

'Do you realize that tomorrow is the one-year anniversary of your open-heart surgery?'

I stop picking up the dinner dishes, steady myself with my hands on the table, and slide into a chair. I am suddenly out of breath, flashbacks of needles and cutting, the heft of despair.

'How could I forget that?'

Sensing my turmoil, Barbara shifts to a positive note.

'All that, and look at you – look at us – six weeks from taking off.'

'I don't want to do *that* again,' dumb and obvious, trying to regain my equilibrium.

'We won't,' beside me now, a hand at the back of my neck. 'It's been almost ten months since you've been in a hospital – other than for tests.'

'I'm not going back,' all the frightened defiance of a seven-year-old.

'You'll get no argument from me.'

We retreat to the safety of evening routine, looking for relief. There are baths to supervise, a load of laundry, and bedtime stories to read. Welcome distractions from an anniversary I'd rather forget.

In the early hours of morning with Barbara asleep beside me, I struggle to get beyond my heart's strange journey, and the unending list of things to do. I ride *Grace* down the length of memory, to our first meeting, years earlier. A single glimpse of her, tied to a seawall in Marathon, Florida, and I am a goner. It is September, 1995 . . .

•••••

'I'D LIKE TO SLEEP ON HER,' to her owner, Bob Williams, an hour after we meet.

'Well, I don't know . . .' he drawls, looking at me with veiled surprise, momentarily off his game.

'Tonight. I know how she looks. I need to see how she *feels*. I'd like to sleep on her tonight.'

'Well,' Bob is studying me intently. *Is this guy loopy?* 'I suppose that could be arranged.'

●●●●●

AFTER GOING OVER EVERY INCH OF *GRACE* with Bob, I call a friend back in Michigan. Jeff is a banker.

'I need your help, Jeff. I've found the boat, the one Barb and I will take out there.' He is already familiar with the plan.

'And you need a loan.'

'A big one, probably more than we qualify for. I'm going to need help to clean us up a bit, make us look presentable.'

'This is the real deal?'

'The real deal, Jeff. She's gorgeous.'

'Let's see what we can do.'

●●●●●

NEXT I CALL BARBARA, home from work by now.

'I found her. Her name is *Grace*.'

I tell her everything I know, her solid construction, her seaworthiness.

'From the sound of your voice' – Barbara knows me – 'she must be pretty.'

'A captain from Annapolis described her as "drop-dead gorgeous". She's the most beautiful sailboat I've ever seen.'

'Easy, boy.'

Barbara cuts me off when I launch into another recital of features.

'If you're *that* sure, I think we should buy her.'

'You've got to see her first.'

'No, I don't. We both know what we want in a boat. If you're sure, I'm sure.'

'This is the purchase of our life. *I* need you to see it, whether *you* do or not.'

She will arrange child care for the kids. I will try to scout up a cheap airline ticket for her.

'Friday?'

'Thursday night would be better.'

•••••

IT TAKES A WHILE TO TRACK Dan Hendrickson down. He is in New York at a conference. The sun is dipping down over Seven Mile Bridge when I finally reach him from a highway pay phone.

'She's yours,' I announce to a bewildered silence.

'I like the sound of it . . . but who is *she*?'

'*Outrageous*,' I wait for a moment, to let it sink in.

'What are you talking about?'

'If you want her . . . I've found our new boat – she's called *Grace*. I want you to have *Outrageous*.'

'Of course I want her,' Dan fumbles, 'but I'm practically broke.'

'We'll deal with the money later. You figure out a price you can afford and a payment you can make. I agree to whatever you come up with.'

'Damn, John . . .'

•••••

ON *GRACE* OVERNIGHT, excitement overrides weariness.
I get up over and over again, padding around in bare feet,
pulling open cabinets, lifting floor boards. I run my hand
over the perfect seams in her trim. I settle into this settee,
then that, studying her from every angle. I poke at the electrical switches gingerly, afraid to try them for fear of blowing
something up. Electricity is still magic to me. I slip up the
companionway and onto her teak decks, and go over her
rigging with a flashlight. I search vainly for a blemish,
anything to take an edge off.

I finally doze off just before dawn, the surrounding
mangroves erupting in a frenzy of anticipation. *It is a done
deal*, I tell myself when I awake. *A done deal.*

When Barbara arrives, it is. Within days we formally
purchase the vessel of our dreams.

•••••

THREE WEEKS FROM DEPARTURE, and we are running out
of time.

David and I are driving back to Grand Rapids after a
weekend of work at the marina. Our conversation about
boys and girls – how it works and when it doesn't – feels
like relief from my obsession with finishing *Grace*. Just
ahead of us, Barbara and Paula are having their own conversation in Paula's van. Katie and Erin have passed out in
the seats behind them, their heads dropping out of view.

With no warning, Paula's van swerves abruptly to the
right, just grazing a car pulled off the road to her left. A
shower of body trim floats up dreamily, and back towards

us. Paula jerks the van back to the left, avoiding the cars in the lane to her right. The airborne trim washes over us as the van careens down into the grassy divider, bouncing violently as it hits the bottom, then up the other side full throttle, across two crowded lanes of onrushing traffic, and down into a deeper ditch, ploughing into the earthen wall that borders the expressway.

I swerve off through an unyielding right lane, braking in a skid on the shoulder. Out of the car now, I run back through the traffic, across the opposing lanes, cars screeching to a halt. My heart erupts as I vault down into the ditch, fearing the worst. Barbara is pushing against her passenger side door, wedging it open.

'The kids! Get the kids!'

I slide open the door into the back seat. They look dazed, hanging at odd angles over their twisted seat belts. Erin breaks into tears at seeing me. I have her now.

'Are you okay?'

'Daddy, what happened?'

'A car accident. Are you okay?'

I am lifting her out, laying her down in the tall grass.

'Stay there. Let me get Katie.'

Back in the van, Katie is motionless.

'Are you okay, sweetie?'

She says nothing, her eyes vague and sleepy, like she was waking up slowly on a school-day morning.

'Are you okay?'

'My stomach hurts.'

'Show me where.' I carefully unsnap her seat belt. A dark bruise is spreading beneath the scuffed skin on her stomach and hip.

'Move your legs for me, Katie. Good. Now your arms. Good. Is your neck okay? Let me lift you out of here.'

I have her up now. Her sleepy warmth offsets the spreading warmth in my chest. I resist the urge to hug her harder, and lay her beside her sister in the grass.

'Just stay still.'

Erin seems shaken but okay. Katie is preternaturally pale and calm.

'Are you okay, Barb?'

A passerby is helping her out. She is bending over the girls. There is wonderment in her eyes, surprise.

'They seem to be okay. Are *you* okay?'

'Yes. Katie seems awfully pale.'

We are surrounded now by people looking to help. An off-duty ambulance man in Bermuda shorts, and his wife, a doctor, with her summer blouse knotted tightly across her midriff. Going over Katie's stomach, probing gently, looking for an internal break. Others are attending to Paula, still sitting motionless in the driver's seat behind us.

'Ambulances are on the way.' And to the girls, 'Be still. Don't move your head.'

I am on my knees between the girls, a hand on either chest, trying to slow my breathing.

'You're okay. You're okay.' Perhaps I am reassuring myself.

I ride to the hospital with Erin and Paula. They are both on backboards, strapped rigidly against the threat of movement. I am focused on Erin, although Paula is more likely to be injured.

'My back,' she says when I ask.

'I'm so sorry,' she insists when our eyes meet, hers full of tears.

'I know, Paula. It could have happened to any of us.'

•••••

WE STRAGGLE OUT OF THE EMERGENCY ROOM in the early morning. Aches and pains, abrasions, nothing more. Paula will not be leaving right away. She has a cracked vertebra in her back. A back brace must be fitted, with several months to full recovery.

'Rethinking your plans?' my brother asks when I tell him what has happened. 'Maybe this is a shot across the bow.'

'Can't get out of here soon enough,' I can grin again. 'Life on shore is too dangerous.'

•••••

IN MY NIGHTMARES the van careens off the road again and again, down into the grass, across the lanes of oncoming traffic. I have lost the woman and the girls I love, and with them, life itself.

I awake with a startle, discover that they have been given new lives.

I have been given a new life also.

•••••

BARBARA AND I STARE ACROSS THE TABLE at one another, used up, mute.

'Girls all set?' I ask numbly.

'Yes. Johanna's taking them out to the park with Shiva, then over to see John Ryan and get some pizza.'

'How about you?' Maybe she can think, talk.

'Nothing left,' Barbara confesses, this from someone who never complains. 'And I don't think I'm going to get it all done by the end of July.' The first time she's said this.

'Me neither,' also a first admission. 'We'll leave when we're ready.'

Barbara may want to feel relief, but she's heard my concerns about early-autumn Northerlies too often.

'Can we get South if we don't leave until the middle of August?' she asks.

'I think so,' the best I can do tonight.

She wisely lets it go.

Barbara revisits the deeper agenda when we are well into a meal that is beginning to revive us.

'Still okay with this, your heart? Last-minute jitters?'

'To tell you the truth, I'm so overwhelmed by all there is to do that I can't see beyond it.' I backpedal then, looking to reassure.

'If I was going to die, I would have . . . out beside that highway.'

Barbara brushes right by me. 'We don't *have* to go.'

'My heart is *not* going to blow up,' with an authority that surprises me. This sounds like confidence.

When she doesn't reply immediately – *let's get off this tack* – I launch into a long recital of safety upgrades to *Grace*: a windlass to protect my heart from anchor-lifting; a single sideband radio for offshore communication and weather; a GPS to tell us where we are; radar to show us where the other guys are; storm sails; a drogue to slow us in the ultimate storm; lazy jacks to make it easier for her to handle our gigantic mainsail.

Barbara listens, but concedes nothing.

'Our ace in the hole' – I need to close the deal – 'is to get you the practice you need to handle *Grace* alone.' No need to spell out how my demise would require it.

'You've got to know that you can get the kids in safely from anywhere. *I've* got to know it.'

Barbara nods with an authority that lets me drop it. We have talked about 'skill sharing' for years, only to fall into more conventional roles in our day-to-day cruising. We have no slack this time, not with my heart.

We lapse into an abrupt silence when my sales pitch is over. Barbara studies my face intently. I don't dare look away.

'So we go?' It is the last time she will ask me.

'We go.'

• • • • •

IT IS AUGUST NINTH, almost a year to the day since my last heart attack. I shield my bloodshot eyes from the sunlight glinting off the surface of White Lake. I am running on empty, round fourteen in a championship bout.

We have closed our offices and packed our professions away. Our house is rented, our remaining possessions banished to the attic. We have said our good-byes, one at a time, rejecting the idea of a grand, dock party send-off. We are too tired to add one more thing to our list.

Piles of boxes still clutter our deck and dock, waiting for a locker to call home. We move about in an explosion of provisions, clearing space to sleep at night. The girls, as usual, are off on a mission. There is a frog to capture and release, a fishing line to inspect, for the big one that never shows up.

Barbara and I have emotional hangovers from all the goodbyes. The ache of wrenching away from John Ryan. An extended separation from a rich community of friends. They will stand in for us on the home front: Dan overseeing our whimsical finances, Paula and David our house rental. John Ryan will troubleshoot when the unexpected crisis erupts. Together they will cover our backs.

My brother and sister, and Barbara's sister Audrey, will provide care and attention to our ageing parents. In my case particularly, this makes leaving possible.

Last night we said goodbye to my housebound parents. Being tired actually helps. I am numb enough to carry it off without breaking down. When we are wrapping it up, I remind my dad of a favourite John Adams quote, something like:

> 'I'll fight wars
> so that my son can own a farm,
> so that his son can do art.'

'We get to do this because of all you and Mom have done. We're standing on your shoulders.'

In spite of his advanced Parkinson's, he gets it, satisfaction flooding his eyes.

Erin notices my silence in the car when we leave.

'Grandpa and Grandma are going to be okay, Daddy.'

Ultimately they are, but it's a long road down.

It all has a dreamlike quality to it this morning. We protect ourselves from what will take us over the edge. The sheer weight of provisioning should deaden the ache of farewell.

I am not sure I will get through this day.

The Sea

*'Yes – the springtimes needed you. Often a star
was waiting for you to notice it. A wave rolled
toward you out of the distant past, or as you
walked under an open window, a violin yielded
itself to your hearing. All this was mission.'*

– Rainer Maria Rilke (translated by Stephen Mitchell)

WE EASE THE GIRLS into their bunks before midnight, finally
collapsing into our berth at 2am. A thunderstorm rolls in
from the Northwest, washing over Whitehall an hour before
dawn. Faint rumblings give way to a roar when it hits. The
wind pins *Grace* to the dock, grinding away at the fenders.

I push aside exhaustion and get up to check. I remove
a companionway slat and look out. Lightning is striking all
around us, the thunder cannoning off *Grace*'s hull and
cabin. Barbara is up now, anxiety overwhelming weariness,
eyes wide with alarm.

'What we don't need is a lightning strike,' grabbing my
arm with both hands.

'It'd be downright beautiful if they weren't so close,' I
counter, trying to take the edge off fear.

The rain comes next, exploding on the deck and cabin top, swamping the cockpit. The short-term assault slackens in minutes. The lightning moves on, across the lake and up the hill. We are left with the abrupt silence of a harsh storm passed. The air is saturated with ozone, the lake given back over to darkness.

Barbara and I stare at each other, dumb with fatigue and relief. We decide to try another hour of rest. I am too agitated to fall asleep, my mind racing with things I still have to do before leaving. I slip out of our berth quietly and pick up where I left off.

Barbara is up shortly, a victim of her own preoccupations. 'Let's get out of here,' she says.

We brush our teeth, throw water in our faces, and brew up some coffee and tea. I turn on the engine and unfasten the dock lines. We pull out of our slip before sunrise, gliding quietly out towards the channel markers. First light follows us from the East.

'We made it,' she exhales as we pass between the first buoys. I reach around the wheel to pull her back to me.

We are too tired to talk. *Grace* rides a line now, down towards the channel into Lake Michigan. Our reverie doesn't last long. Within minutes the engine alarm comes on, a shrill warning of trouble. I check the oil pressure and water temperature gauges. The latter is into the red zone.

'Shut the engine down.' I race forward to drop the anchor.

The clatter of the escaping chain is almost more than my frazzled nerves can take. I kneel at the bow, holding onto the lifelines. The ache in my chest reminds me that I have forgotten my morning medication. When the chain plays out, I secure the anchor line to the samson post.

Nobody said it would be easy.

I move back into the cockpit and down through the companionway. I remove the engine cover. Barbara follows me, picking up the house flashlight on the way.

'There it is,' taking the light from her hand. 'The belt on the water pump broke.'

'Big problem?'

'No, just a pain in the neck. Great start,' I add, immediately wanting to take it back. I open a cabinet to get my tools.

'We're on our way, John. That's the big thing.'

The girls sleep through the belt replacement project. They wake an hour later as we make our way through the White Lake Channel into Lake Michigan. Another hour finds us up the coast to the North, motor-sailing in the beginnings of a light breeze. I shift into neutral to see if the wind is ready to take over. The transmission doesn't downshift.

'Not again'. I motion Barbara back behind the wheel and again retreat to the engine compartment. After repeated attempts to hand-shift, the transmission finally slips into neutral. It won't cooperate when I attempt to shift it back into forward, finally catching on my fifth attempt.

'Damn,' quietly this time. My response will not be lost on Barbara and the kids. We are three hours and two crises into our long-anticipated trip.

'We can sail up to Pentwater' – all eyes are focused on me – 'and nurse her in. We'll get a mechanic to look at the transmission.'

Erin immediately goes to the bottom line: 'Are we going to be okay?'

'We're going to be fine, Erin.' I remind myself that it's true. Mechanical problems are just mechanical problems; weariness just weariness.

'Do you think we ought to head back?' Barbara asks, out of earshot of the girls. 'Pentwater is 30 miles up the coast . . .'

'It makes sense logistically, but not emotionally. We've made our break. Let's go with it.'

Whatever her misgivings, she doesn't disagree.

The girls are up at the bow now, excited about being underway. 'Finally!' makes its way back to Barbara and me in the cockpit.

'I'm with them,' Barbara nods, just the hint of a grin, then a weary but irrepressible smile.

I smile back. 'Me, too.'

●●●●●

THE NEWS ISN'T GOOD IN PENTWATER. The transmission will have to be removed and rebuilt. It will cost us four days and six hundred dollars.

'An inauspicious beginning.'

Barbara isn't buying it.

'It's a good thing we caught it now. Besides, we can use a few days' rest.'

She's right on both counts. We put our four days to good use. I replace cracked lines in the propane system and get the galley pump working. I install a new sump pump in the head. We get Katie off to a dentist when a tooth erupts unexpectedly.

'We just had her in for a check-up,' Barbara protests.

Katie has a baby tooth extracted.

Friends visit us, unwilling to let go. We play miniature golf with the kids each afternoon. We spend lazy hours over meals and take nightly walks to the ice cream parlour. Most importantly, we sleep. We wake up, roll over and sleep some more.

By the time we leave Pentwater, we are beyond the first shock of departure.

'Rested enough to know how tired we are,' Barbara observes.

We stop in Manistee on our way North, leaving our friends Barry and Dana tearful on the dock. Their tears are contagious. It is a rich life we are stepping back from, to check out the undiscovered part.

We have not sailed any distance since our single, abbreviated cruise last summer. It shows. We wake up during an early morning squall in Frankfort harbour to discover that we have dragged our anchor. Two days later, we get caught in another blow, north of Charlevoix. We can see it rolling in as we motor down the channel towards Lake Michigan. It is howling out of the Southwest, grey and steely, snapping at the halyards.

'Are you sure?' Barbara asks.

'No, but it's supposed to clear later.'

This is not how we like to make decisions, backs against the wall. We are too aware of the calendar. Autumn is closing in.

'I think we should go for it.'

I put two reefs in the main, and shorten the foresail. Then it is on us, hard and unyielding. Although the wind never breaks forty, it doesn't let up, even for a minute. It is a single, seamless barrage, just blowing without taking a breath. The waves, already large, are ominous within an hour, their thick torsos blasting away at the hull, their steep peaks clawing at us. Have we angered them by coming out? *We warned you, but you didn't listen. Now we'll have at you.*

We get thrown around a bit.

It has been two years and a compromised heart since we've been in any serious weather. It will take a while to relax down into whatever confidence remains, in *Grace* and in ourselves.

I've been here before, I remind myself as Barbara and the kids retreat below, but my body remembers more recent insults. I am too aware of the heaviness in my chest.

'You okay?' Barbara checks and checks again. 'Are you too cold?' She doesn't need to mention my heart.

I'm still me, I tell myself.

But everything has changed.

●●●●●

RELAXATION DEEPENS IN THE ENSUING WEEKS. Lazy, late-summer days usher us down through Lake Huron and into Lake Erie. Katie and Erin thrive on our undivided attention. We know better than to think this will always be the case. They still enjoy being with us, almost as much as we enjoy them.

Barbara initiates them into 'boat school.' She has hammered out a year's goals and objectives with Paula, who is a teacher. We want to supplement mainline academics with the physical confidence that can only be learned in action. 'Spend time before the big screen' we tell others, turning off the TV for good. We hope travel will give them real life exposure to diverse cultures, living history and geography. Mathematics will be applied, science natural. And the love of literature that comes from being curled up with a book at the end of the day. They seem enthused at these first ventures into learning afloat.

In spite of time pressures, we meander along, pausing for several frenetic days at Cedar Point Amusement Park. Friends meet us there, taking advantage of our open invitation.

We are easing into a new life. We remind ourselves when we get wistful that we have burned no bridges irreparably. I have to stay healthy. The girls need to learn and thrive. We must live frugally. It has to be fun. If the pieces fall into place, there is a lot of world to explore. If not, we have a home to return to in a place that we love, jobs that we value, friends and family that we miss already. The Great Lakes will still be here, to sail for weeks at a time.

The nature of adventure is that you don't know how it turns out. *Don't have to*, I remind myself again and again.

This is it. Barbara moves gracefully around the deck, suntanned and fit, glancing up at the sails, and out for a long time at the horizon.

Katie pops out of the cabin, azure eyes ablaze. She gestures at her radio, and asks, 'You know what this song is named?

'*Take the Long Way Home*,' she answers before I can.

'That's what we're doing, isn't it, Dad . . . taking the long way home?' I smile, a casualty of her wide-eyed clarity.

'Yes, Katie, the long way home.

'In another, very real way, we are already home.'

What I don't tell her is that her mother is my home,

she and her sister with their spindly arms and playful fingers, her broad-shouldered brother and our brown dog, Shiva, this sleek, strong *Grace* of ours, and the freshwater surge beneath us.

•••••

'Is it true what they say, that you guys are going to sail around the world?'

The earnest young attendant at the gas dock has already told me about his college career: senior year, business administration. When he turns the questions on me, I'm taken by surprise.

'That's a possibility. We're taking it one day at a time, making it up as we go.'

'No plan?' He is at attention.

'John Lennon used to say that "life is what happens to you while you're busy making other plans". Something like that . . .'

He brushes by John Lennon, blank-faced and insistent. 'You must be great sailors, to do that with kids.'

'That'd be nice, but it's a stretch. We're B-sailors at best. Probably C+.'

'Ah, c'mon!'

'If we wait until we're good enough, we might never go.'

Later, as we're motoring out into Lake Erie, I smile at the 'great sailor' allusion. I've grabbed at enough brass rings for several lifetimes. The last thing I need is another competitive sport. I'll settle for being halfway competent. *Safe* would be good.

Nor will we ever have the best appointed, most pristine boat in the harbour. With my primitive technical skills, it normally takes three times the effort to do half the job. For every subtraction from my ongoing 'to do' list, I make two additions. Shipshape is out of reach.

I'll have to settle for *safe*.

We simply want to sail where we haven't been, out beyond what we know. Look around, check out the larger territory. Do more than know *about* it.

If we're lucky, we'll put some ocean under us, and wake up in some beautiful places.

• • • • •

THE WIND SHIFTS TO THE SOUTHWEST as the sun sets, filling the sails with fresh insistence. *Grace* surges ahead, settling in at just under seven knots. The purple horizon stands in stark contrast to the belching towers of a power plant on Lake Erie's southern shore.

I ask Barbara to turn on the tricolour light. Post-dinner warmth wafts up into the cockpit. The clatter of pots and pans rides the updraft, the re-energized enthusiasm of Katie and Erin. The debate over the value or superficiality of make-up, begun over dinner in the cockpit, continues, no let-up in sight. Erin cackles with delight as Katie howls her indignation. Barbara's laughter punctuates the charge and countercharge, clearly relishing the give and take.

Whatever else falls away, the hard-bitten habits of sisterhood survive the transition from shore to sea.

Many other land-based habits are slipping away, one month into our trip. As darkness closes in with its early fall chill, I sift through remnants of departure . . .

• • • • •

I AM GROUSING ABOUT IN THE FLOTSAM of the V-berth, growling out loud about the 'damn keys' I have misplaced, hopeful of attracting Barbara's assistance. She doesn't take the bait. Suddenly I stop and begin to laugh.

'What's so funny?' Laughter is apparently more invitational than complaint.

'It doesn't matter. I have lost my keys, and it doesn't matter.'

We have already left the cars, house and office to which they gain entry. I have stepped back from everything but my family and the good boat *Grace*. Rather than feeling diminished, I feel free.

• • • • •

SIMPLE IS NOT THE SAME THING as easy. I rub my hands together for warmth, shifting position in search of relief for my complaining back. It is not midnight yet, and I am already chilled. We plan to ride this developing Westerly through the night, at least another 90 miles to Dunkirk, New York.

The night's procession of kisses complete, it's dark below deck. I resolve not to wake Barbara until she's had several hours of sleep. Her day has been more challenging than mine. She juggles the chores of teacher, mother, and all-purpose crew member. When I rouse her, she will be up and dressed quickly, good-natured at the prospect of a long watch with a cloudless, star-strewn sky. Barbara loves to sail at night.

Ours are long-established routines. I am pretty good at cooking up schemes and adventures. She breathes life into them, does more than go along to please me. She hangs in there when Mr Big Stuff gets scuffed up and demoralized – during our first sojourn through the Mediterranean and Caribbean, and throughout the ongoing ordeal with my heart. And she's out here again, five hundred miles into this half-baked venture.

The thought of my good fortune warms me.

Shore reality shrinks to a narrow line of lights, miles off starboard, between the silver and black undulation of Lake Erie and the immensity of the September sky. It is a thin, fragile slice, clearly the smallest portion.

Out ahead is the shimmering alley the moon makes as she comes over the horizon. Not a full moon any more, but close. She goes from orange to cream-coloured in the hour after rising, gives light, but little to dilute the cold. Watching her, the cold matters less.

As the night and the light take me in, I let go. Thoughts fall away, and the weariness. In time, maybe the cold. Even the sailor, if I am lucky. Leaving only the moon and the water, the quiet abundance of the moment.

At 2am I wake Barbara. She pulls on polypropylene, wool and foul-weather gear. She makes some tea, grabs her trusty radio, and climbs cheerfully behind the helm. The moon is high in the sky now. Barbara enters the zone.

Down below, I pull off my clothes. I inhale a peanut butter sandwich that would make Rick cringe. I fluff up the pillow. I listen to the water rushing by the hull, the hum of the whirling propeller. *Grace* is on the prowl. However tired, I am wide awake.

My mind wanders back to the lost keys, all that's been put in abeyance in order to go to sea again. I recall a Zen poem:

> *'My barn having burned to the ground,*
> *I can now see the moon.'*

For a while I am stepping away from shore-based reality, in order to see the moon.

•••••

I RETURN TO THE HELM SHORTLY AFTER DAWN. Barbara reports a dreamy watch, with ample accompaniment by the moon. After a short exchange, she heads below to get some much-needed sleep. The wind gradually clocks around, strengthening as it becomes more westerly. I am having difficulty keeping the genoa full in the following wind.

I shift to wing and wing. In this configuration – a full main eased out on one side of the mast, a full genoa on the other – I must pay close attention to the wheel. Any deviation off-centre can result in the wind getting behind a sail. If the genoa backsails, we have a temporary mess. If I backsail the main, we flirt with disaster – the possibility of a jibe. Many sailing deaths occur when a boat unintentionally jibes, the backsailed main sweeping the deck with a skull-cracking swing of the boom. I secure the boom with a boom vang.

The kids sleep until mid-morning, recovering from the excitement of Cedar Point. They make their way into the cockpit for a morning kiss, then hunch over bowls of cereal. Katie, ever interested in speed, consults the GPS. We are edging up on nine knots now.

'That's pretty fast, Dad.'

'Time to get your life jackets on.'

It is pretty fast. I regularly glance back over my shoulder, seeking assurance from the clear, sunny skies. They carry no warning of winds that jump from fifteen to twenty-five knots. The waves quickly follow suit. They double from four to eight feet, then start the cycle again.

I am working hard now, with a vague cramp spreading up into my neck.

I keep expecting the wind to moderate. With this forecast and these sunny skies, it certainly will.

It doesn't.

Instead, the wind continues to mount, and with it the following swells and our speed. I have been tricked by the warm sun, the almost languid blue it paints the surface. Caribbean colours with a North Sea twist.

'Put those safety harnesses on, girls.'

I wait too long to wake Barbara. By the time I do, we are hurtling along just within control. The swells are continuing to build, now at an alarming rate. Though they are helping us rocket along, they will turn on us unmercifully if we get sideways to them. I struggle to keep from backdrafting a sail. I fight the helm as each breaker overtakes us, inviting a lurch to a broadside.

'I'm sorry,' I confess the obvious when Barbara comes up into the cockpit. 'I waited too long.' Her eyes register alarm as they dart from swells to sails and back.

'I thought it would settle. It just keeps building.'

Barbara pulls on a life jacket.

'We've got to shorten the sails — without throwing the boat out of balance and broaching.'

'How?' She is struggling to stay calm.

'Let's see if you and Katie can furl in the genoa — you'll

have to use a winch – while I keep us from getting side-swiped by a swell. Then we can turn into the wind, get the main reefed.'

I shout instructions while struggling to control the wheel. Barbara and the girls are starting to furl in the genoa when a cam cleat on the traveller explodes. The gunshot retort breaks my concentration long enough to get thrown off balance by a following swell. The boom rockets up over the cabin top and is stuck amidship by the boom vang. *Grace* lurches broadside into the swells and rolls onto her side, unable to right herself. The sails are holding her over now, her toerail buried in the water. Two roguish broadsides roll her over even further, water cascading into the cockpit.

Barbara grabs the kids and pins them to the high side of the cockpit. Three pair of eyes register panic. For a second I am in entirely new territory, so surprised I have no idea how to save us. I reach down and switch on the engine, and redline the throttle, trying to generate enough speed to turn towards the wind and rob it of its power.

My heart joins the rebellion as *Grace* lurches forward – a slow motion dip towards the wind – and spills the worst of it off the sails. They erupt in a clatter as *Grace* staggers back towards equilibrium. She shakes the foam out of her genoa, and stands almost upright.

'Take the wheel and keep her on this heading!' Barbara moves without hesitation to the helm.

'Help me furl in the genoa, girls.' I wrap the furling line around my right hand. *I can do this.*

The girls spring into action, effort overwhelming fear. I reach into reserves I've not dared tap since my first heart attack. I hand-over-hand the furling line, growling as we bring in the foresail. I try to shake the pain out of my hands after I secure the line. No time for the blisters that erupt in each palm.

'You're doing great,' I shout to Barbara. 'Keep us directly on the wind.'

I move up the deck to drop the main, grabbing at the mast to steady myself. I try to breathe away the tightness gathering in the centre of my chest. *Slow and easy*. However boisterous the wind and the waves, we should be okay now. When I get the main down, we can motor out beyond the encroaching shallows, then across the wind into Dunkirk Harbour.

An hour later, we nudge up to the city dock, passing lines to a cluster of onlookers.

'Pretty rough out there?' A leathery old hand extended.

'Thank you. And yes,' a first smile, 'it was pretty rough.'

• • • • •

WE ARE SECURE NOW, with *Grace* tied up against the pilings. The girls shift quickly towards excitement.

'We did it, Dad!'

'We sure did,' wanting to follow them out of dread. 'You guys did great.'

'Yes, you did,' Barbara enjoins, shifting gears from whatever else she's thinking.

She looks over, something like relief.

'You, too, Captain.'

I take a deep breath and exhale. Although her calm is reassuring, I have not recovered from the adrenaline overload. I go mechanically about the job of hitching up sheets, coiling lines, flaking the crudely wrapped main.

We are safe, I keep reminding myself, but damage has been done. The confidence that has been working its way back into me is in shreds. I didn't anticipate the exuberance of the wind and the swells it would fashion in Lake Erie's shallows. I put us at risk – not just myself, but Barbara and the girls.

Barbara senses my distress as the afternoon drains into dusk.

'You got us through it. And your heart didn't blow up.' When I say nothing, 'If you can take that, you can take a lot.'

I nod agreement, but cannot muster a smile. I am shaken in a way I have not been since leaving the hospital a year ago. Fear has re-entered me, those seconds when I was paralysed and didn't know what to do. The place of no control, all the dread I have lived with, detritus of a wounded heart.

Have I lost something, more than I thought?

•••••

WE MUST GET BACK ON THE HORSE.

The following day we ride a mild Northwesterly the forty miles to Buffalo. Later that night I am visited by more immediate demons, transfixed in front of a television at an Italian restaurant as Notre Dame gets thrashed by Michigan State. Disappointment almost feels like relief.

Physical equilibrium returns: a mast to take down, three hundred miles of beauty to navigate in the Erie Canal. We put the mast back up at a marina on the Hudson. Several more sunny September days usher us down to New York

City for a short stay. Long walks help, as does the cacophony of the streets.

We have made our way to the sea, but with an unwelcome stowaway. Uncertainty travels with me everywhere I go.

•••••

AFTER SEVERAL DAYS IN NEW YORK, a passable weather forecast releases us. We spend the morning battening things down and stowing fresh provisions away. We unfasten the dock lines just after noon, and catch the ebbing current out into New York Harbour. There are freighters to avoid, and the ferries charging to and from Staten Island. Two monster racing boats dart back and forth, putting equipment, sails and crew to the test. Are these America's Cup contenders? New York never fails to amaze.

As the skyscrapers recede behind us, the tide kicks in, speeding us out towards the Atlantic. We round the point at Sandy Hook late in the afternoon and head South in a westerly breeze. Warmth flees with the sun, leaving us with the penetrating cold of early autumn. We shorten our watch schedule. I chill quickly and recover slowly these days. Is it more than weakened circulation, more than the price of medicinally thinned blood? Is fear an element in this easy constriction?

By dawn, we are eighty-five miles from New York, twenty-eight miles from the mouth of the Delaware Bay. The wind has turned against us, the Westerlies sliding to the Southwest and intensifying. The bluster builds, cold and on the nose. It begins to drizzle, then to rain. With each tack we seem to lose speed, dropping below five knots, then four. The swells are building. We slip below three knots. I turn on the engine, but it doesn't help much. The wind-driven rain finds its way into every crease and crevice, drains me of resolve.

We slog along stolidly, labouring but not in danger. In an unfamiliar role reversal, I ask Barbara, 'Do you think we ought to head back, duck into Atlantic City?'

She thinks about it for only a moment, answering in a firm but even voice.

'I don't think we should give away what we've already got. If you're feeling okay, I'd like to push on.'

I nod my half-hearted agreement, aware that my willingness to look for shelter has less to do with the weather than with my internal malaise. There's a hitch in my step now, a hesitation that wasn't there before Dunkirk.

Late in the afternoon we fight our way into Cape May, competing with an outrushing tide. The sun breaks through during an hour-long search for a place to anchor. Warmth works its way into my knotted neck and shoulders, the quiet satisfaction of our first Atlantic passage of this trip.

We drop anchor and secure it. It drags before dusk.

'This area is too exposed,' Barbara suggests, emerging from the cabin with a weather report.

'Big winds on the way.'

●●●●●

'I've MISSED YOU.' Barbara reaches around me as I brush my teeth, her fingers splayed over my chest.

'Me, too,' trying unsuccessfully to contain the toothpaste dripping off my chin.

We have melted down thoroughly over time, a vague longing when night watches keep us apart. Each of us grabs what rest we can when the other is on watch, to avoid the sleep deprivation that can put us at risk.

The primitive intensity of these overnight passages – solitary hours at the helm, snatches of sleep in an empty berth – ratchets up anticipation for next harbour's reunion. This reunion, this night. The hand that cradles a cup of Bailey's, the dimpled wrist; those soft eyes and that easy smile, the unimpeachable language of the body.

The nervousness of the early days is gone now, the cleverness and clumsiness, the fidgeting. We talk for an hour after the girls are asleep, incapable of evasion. We pause when the wind interrupts, check to make sure the anchor is still set. The bonfire tenderness remains. Everything we have of worth, our family and our dreams, rolls out ahead of that unearned warmth.

'I'm crazy about you, girl.'

We are crawling up into our V-berth bunk.

'You are why I am alive.'

•••••

WHEN THE WIND CALMS DOWN, we set sail up Delaware Bay. It is very shallow after the ocean.

'Stay in between the buoys, big guy,' Barbara is well aware of my ranginess.

'Dot-to-dot,' Erin chimes in.

'Life on a boat full of women,' I complain. 'Be nice. Keep your head down. Stay between the lines.'

'Give me a break!' Katie joins the fray.

Being the only male aboard is a pretty cushy ride, 'a

lifelong fantasy' Barbara calls it. 'Captain John and his all-girl crew.'

I undoubtedly get better than I deserve. My part of the bargain is to keep everyone safe and happy. The success of our cruise, its range and duration, depends on it. *Grace* is too small a place for even one malcontent. Like shore life, only more so.

'Don't you get it?' I used to ask particularly intransigent clients. 'If you win and she loses, you lose. You're in it together. If he's unhappy and you're not, it will spill over onto you.'

Life in close quarters. Enlightened self-interest.

It is well after dark when we find the entrance to the C&D Canal. We have to backtrack to locate it, lost in a maze of competing lights. In the early hours of morning we drop anchor in the tiny boat harbour at Chesapeake City.

We sleep deep into the next day, an exhalation after a time-bound sprint. By late afternoon I am at an outdoor table overlooking the harbour, hunched over an article I am writing.

'Saw you come in this morning,' a tousled, white-haired nod in the direction of *Grace*. 'Where you headed?'

Each answer calls forth another question.

'Any close calls?' dredges up our misadventure at Dunkirk.

'With a boom that long' – he tips his hand a bit – 'and that mast, you pack a lot of mainsail.'

'Yup.'

'Can't wait too long to get those reefs in.'

'I did at Dunkirk.' Apparently we both know.

'A lifelong struggle,' when he does not reply. 'Not so good at shortening my sails.'

'Me neither,' a gleam in his eye. He grins broadly now, a missing tooth, crevices deepening around his mouth and eyes.

'Most of us probably reef the sails too quickly in our shore lives,' he concedes, 'but there's a place for it out there.'

'Would have helped up in Erie,' I admit, comfortable with the room he has given me.

When he shuffles on I mull over a lifelong reluctance to shorten the sails, the commotion of it. A smile belies thoroughly mixed feelings.

Done that, I conclude. *I live in a different place now.*

Reefing the sails is a small trade-off for a safe and happy crew, a partial ticket to a long cruise.

Besides, the old guy is right. I can reef my sails without reefing my life.

• • • • •

WE STAY IN ANNAPOLIS LONGER THAN WE PLANNED. The boat show, a town that we love. We squeeze in a two-week trip back to Michigan to see John Ryan and our parents.

It's more than that, probably, more than just camping at anchor, soaking up the warm Maryland autumn. I have an uncomfortable new sense of vulnerability, exposed at Dunkirk, and unresolved.

The head breaks during the last week of October. It takes three days to tear down, secure parts, and rebuild.

'Isn't yachting glamorous?' I mutter to Barbara, glancing up from its caked entrails.

The day I reinstall it, Barbara takes the girls off the boat to the library. By midafternoon, I am rushing to finish other last-minute jobs. I lean deep into the bilge to tighten the packing gland on the drive shaft. When the pipe wrench slips, the bridge of my nose smacks into the teak framing, a knockout punch.

I shake my head to clear it, with a string of sailor's epithets. I open my eyes to find blood flying hither and yon.

This is serious. I am alone on *Grace*, moored in the harbour. I press a towel over the cut long enough to slow it, then remove the towel momentarily to survey the damage in the mirror. I have a deep, semi-circular gash high on the bridge of my nose. A flap of skin is laid back unceremoniously. I reapply pressure, but not before the gushing begins in earnest again.

This is how a haemophiliac must feel. The front of my shirt is covered with blood now, dripping from the soaked towel. 'Damn skinny blood,' I mutter out loud, fully aware that it is keeping me alive.

I grab a second towel and an emergency kit with bandages of every size. I stumble up into the cockpit, stop to regain my balance, then slide awkwardly over the side into the dinghy. I press the towel to my nose as hard as I can tolerate, until I am dizzy with the pain. I start the outboard motor after several awkward attempts. Within minutes I roar into the main basin in downtown Annapolis, to the horror of onlookers lounging on benches in the afternoon sun.

'Must look like a serial killer,' I grumble from under the bloody towel. People rewrap half-finished sandwiches, turn away in revulsion. Some get up and walk away.

A clot of teenage boys looks on in utter fascination as I roll out of the dinghy and onto the concrete steps, trying to hold the dinghy line, the bandages, and the offending towel.

'Aagh!' one shouts in a testosterone-laced combination of disgust and awe, like when somebody *really* throws up at a party.

'You're messed up, mister,' is the closest he can get to empathy.

A tide of sightseers recedes as I walk up the steps. Some pretend not to see. A few stay, staunch Samaritans willing to help. Two off-duty nurses step in, swallowing their apprehension long enough to assist. Blood has soaked through the towel now, and is running down my arm, dripping off my right elbow. A crime scene.

I try to explain what happened, to cooperate with their fumbling good intentions. I realize I don't have a clue what I want, or what to do.

A greying businessman moves in, prepared to take over. 'We've got to get you to the hospital.'

Hospital? Other accidents flash before me, needles, stitching, the inevitable overreaction to my sorry heart. I look at him with my own brand of horror, realizing I may have walked into a trap.

'I don't want to go to the hospital,' I protest sternly, to the astonishment of my attendees. I am also surprised by the intensity of my response. *I really don't want to go to the hospital*.

'I've spent too much time there,' I explain to the squinted eyes, the scepticism.

'You've got to get that stitched up,' one of the nurses

says supportively, none of the take-charge in her voice or demeanour.

'Absolutely!' the unranked colonel seems offended by my lack of good sense.

'I'll call an E-Unit,' he barks, and marches off across the busy street, gesturing at the traffic, and into a nearby restaurant.

'Don't,' I shout after him, to no apparent avail. 'I'm not going,' I announce to those around me.

'I'll take care of this myself,' reassuring them now. 'I'll go to the hospital if I can't stop the bleeding.'

A quick perusal, nothing but disbelief.

'Thank you, all of you. Thank you very much.' I am moving now, off to the right, running to get clear, to escape the most determined of my helpers, those who might physically try to stop me. Past the benches, around the corner of the seawall, sprinting now, I don't know where, *away*, to do I don't know what.

Across the street now, *watch the Audi*, bright drops of blood defying gravity in the afternoon sun, between parked cars, partially glancing off a meter, down the pavement to the right, people recoiling, through a doorway on impulse, a favourite coffee shop, and back towards its toilet, past two customers with their backs to me, a clerk with eyes glued to the mysteries of the cash register, down the darkened hallway and through the unlocked door to safety. I click the lock. *A clean getaway*.

I slip a nitro under my tongue, for the mounting ache in my chest. I sit down for a moment. *Breathe*. Another nitro. Keep the towel on that nose.

For twenty minutes I operate in this urban war zone.

I reorder the skin flap. With paper towels and a lot of pressure the bleeding slows to a trickle. Each time I let off, the seepage begins again, the seam opening with the flow. More pressure.

'Damn, that hurts.' *Be patient.*

'I'm sorry, I am sick in here,' when someone tries the door. One more nitro, the beginnings of a medicine-induced headache.

'I'm going to be in here for a while,' when the door-knob rattles again. 'I'm sorry.'

I am gradually able to quench the bleeding. I tape a homemade pressure pack in place. Some blood soaks through, then apparently stops seeping. Moving in slow motion, I clean the bathroom as well as I can. I stuff the blood-soaked towel deep into the trash bin, covering it with used paper towels. I dab the blood off my face and neck, slowly wash my hands and arms. I can do nothing for the shirt except drape the second towel over myself. A new look.

'Don't break open,' I caution my throbbing nose.

I open the door furtively, relieved to find the hallway empty. I walk past the counter with feigned nonchalance, avoiding eye contact with the employee who is studying me. In seconds I am back on the sidewalk, carefully retracing a trail of blood spots back toward the boat basin. *Slowly,* I remind myself. And to my nose, *don't break open.*

The assembled knot has long dissolved, leaving me with a fresh collection of strollers and the still warm afternoon. I gingerly sit on the seawall, shift sideways, hoist my feet up, and ease myself down, my face to the forgiving sun. *Let it dry for a while, coalesce.*

I drift into a low-grade stupor, adrenaline withdrawal and relief. *A clean getaway*, with conviction this time, and a first cautious smile.

• • • • •

'DAD, WHAT HAPPENED TO YOU?' It is Katie, standing over me, blocking the sun.

'I'm okay, I'm okay,' I assure Erin as she recoils from my nose and my blood-soaked shirt.

'Had an accident,' to Barbara as she approaches.

• • • • •

THE WARM AFTERNOONS ARE GROWING SHORTER, with the first stir of cold from the North. Halloween is a frigid celebration of creatures and delight. The girls' bags overflow with sweets, 'enough to take us through to spring'.

Chesapeake Bay is greyer every day.

In early November, we motor by the Naval Academy, out of the protection of the harbour. We hoist the sails and drift south on a light breeze. In the late afternoon a raw haze blows in, and with it, acceleration.

I struggle with the erratic windvane, unable to coax it into holding a downwind course. It is a mystery that will go largely unsolved for months.

It feels good to be underway, free of anchor inertia. Only the deepening chill alarms me, the ache it evokes in my chest. I hope we haven't overstayed.

Despite resolutions to the contrary, it is dark before we creep up into the river at Patuxent. We resolve to drop future anchors before the opaque confusion of night. It is a pledge we have made before.

A blanket of frost drops over us, by dawn a blustery rain.
'Nice day to go sailing.'

'We can stay here and wait it out,' Barbara offers.

'I don't think we should give away any more time. It's getting late.'

'You're going to freeze out there.'

As usual, Barbara is right. When we lose ground in the face of an insistent headwind on our first tack, I consider retreat. The wet is finding its way into every seam. Forty minutes, and already shivering. But we must get down to Norfolk somehow, to prepare for the challenge of Cape Hatteras.

'I'm going to need something hot,' I tell Barbara when she suggests turning back.

I don't have to repeat the request. Hourly rations of hot chocolate, soup, coffee and grilled cheese sandwiches stave off the chill somewhat, and slow the competition going on in my chest. That we have sailed on feels like a victory when we finally drop anchor at Kilnarnack. It is 10.30, deep into the uncertainty of night. Again.

The rain has blown through by morning, but the deck is caked with frost.

'One more leg to Norfolk,' I announce to a shivering crew when I come back down the companionway.

'Great, Dad,' Katie responds. 'But we've got to get a heater.'

The cold is taking a toll.

By 10pm we are off the harbour entrance into Norfolk. We again have trouble sorting the channel markers out of the myriad lights on the horizon.

'Barbara, I need your help out here. You too, girls. I need your eyes.'

We finally set the anchor after 2am, in a pond just off the river into Hampton. I know it is an easy entrance, but I am just too tired to try.

'This is where mistakes get made,' I concede to Barbara, who has been encouraging me to wait.

'It'll be easier in the morning.'

• • • • •

WE MOTOR UP THE RIVER shortly after noon. Hot showers lift our spirits, and take the edge off the epidemic chill.

'God, I hope it warms up,' I tell Barbara.

'I hope we haven't waited too long.'

It's Hatteras she's talking about. There are hundreds of square miles of shallows and shoals out there, over which the Gulf Stream races in a rampage back to the open waters of the North Atlantic. A fifteen-knot Northerly into the face of this current makes a real mess of the seascape. Thirty knots and you've got the makings of a disaster. There are a thousand rotting hulls out there, offering testimony with their gaping mouths.

Memories of Hatteras are all too available to me in the dark, the steam from our breath wafting up towards the overhead hatch. It was here that Dan, Barry and I got caught in a storm on our first Atlantic crossing. I remember too vividly getting our brains beaten out, and losing our electronics.

Overhead, the North wind howls, the resolve-rendering shudder in the rigging. Hatteras is tattooed indelibly on me, down in the memory of cells. Nine years later, it still rattles and shakes within this sleepless night.

• • • • •

DAYS ARE PILING UP NOW, AND NIGHTS, each more brutal than the last. In spite of the infusion of fresh blood – a friend, Kirsten Sloan, arrives for an extended visit – the sustained Northerlies are taking a toll.

Still bearing the scar of Dunkirk, our concern about Hatteras mounts perceptively with each passing day and congeals into dread in the icy hours of night. Barbara and I resolve to talk our way through it. I confess my heightened sense of physical vulnerability. She admits to a parallel set of fears, the grainy residue of engine stalls when we have taken on bad fuel, the forecasted fifteen-knot wind that erupts to a battering thirty. She has deep anxieties about taking over in a serious storm, were my heart to take me out of play.

Whenever we are in danger of being swamped altogether, we remind ourselves that we have been sailing for thirteen years and have a sixteen-month Mediterranean and Caribbean stint under our belts. I have sailed across the Atlantic single handed. Neither of us mentions that this was before my heart problems.

We talk intermittently through several freezing nights, waiting futilely for a weather window. In day after day of deepening cold and strengthening Northerlies, the fear we have hoped to dissipate grows to almost paralyzing proportions. We discuss the possibility of dropping our mast and 'going inside', down the intracoastal waterway, rather than sailing 'outside' in the Atlantic.

While we huddle for encouraging warmth in Hampton, the Atlantic waits just outside the mouth of the Chesapeake, cold and impersonal, a deeper shade of slate with every lost degree of temperature.

•••••

'WE CAN DO THIS, BARBARA.' I am talking to myself. 'I know we can.'

'Let's go.'

The cold has not retreated yet, but the Northerlies have weakened. The girls are safely asleep in a Virginia Beach motel, stage one in a series of adventures that Kirsten has planned for them. They will join us in Beaufort, North Carolina in three days, when we have Hatteras behind us.

'You have fun. We'll see you soon.'

'You have fun, too, Dad.'

Late-life children will either kill you or keep you alive. Either way, they will stretch your otherwise calcifying point of view.

'You have fun, too,' I repeat to Barbara, as dock line knots defy our numb fumbling.

'How did we get so lucky?'

•••••

WE RIDE THE TIDE OUT OF NORFOLK HARBOUR, and make our way between the buoys into the Chesapeake. At the mouth of the bay, we begin a long, lazy arc to the South, out into the Atlantic. Church bells toll in the distance. The offshore light at Hatteras is 110 miles away. The contrary Gulf Stream will make us work for it.

We are relieved with our decision to do this stretch without the girls. Time to work on the skill-sharing we have long discussed. Spend a few days together, just the two of us. Spare them the wear and tear if we get caught out here.

Barbara takes the work out of passages. She fights me

for equal time at the helm. She uses the time she would otherwise spend with the girls to rustle up a parade of edible surprises, piping hot and welcome.

A mild Westerly kicks in, eases us into the evening. The cold makes no concessions. Clouds rob us of any solace the setting sun might offer. We huddle behind the dodger for cover when darkness brings a further drop in temperature. The night stretches empty and ominous ahead of us. The chill calls blood's warmth to the surface, an ache in my chest reminding me that there is not enough to go around. The unwelcome sense of vulnerability enshrouds me, the bracing that is fear. *Keep moving. Keep warm. Deal with it.*

I resort to feistiness, a surviving habit of adolescence. Better to be mad than sad, or worse yet, scared. The contraction only ratchets up the pain. I search the horizon for solutions. Finding none, I can only sail.

Barbara relieves me at 2am, taking the most frigid watch of the night. She holds my face in warm hands, then sends me below. She rouses me just before daybreak.

'Come up here, just for a minute.' We stand together – is it warmer? – as the light of Hatteras indents the horizon, competing with that larger first light for attention.

'Didn't want you to miss it,' she whispers excitedly.

'Now go back to bed.'

•••••

We round the light off the Hatteras Shoals in the early afternoon. To our relief, the weather has become uncharacteristically mild. We are still eighty miles from the tip of Frying Pan Shoals, another thirty or so to Beaufort, North

Carolina. But Hatteras is behind us now, the shallows that can spell disaster. The sun is trying to break through the clouds, that first longed-for hint of the South's hospitality.

A simple, extended glance prompts a hasty extinction of the sails, a quick but exhilarating celebration below decks. We straggle back into the cockpit, pulling on clothes, giggling like a couple of naughty kids. After raising the sails, we languish over a long, drawn-out lunch. Snack and doze. Dolphins arrive as if on cue, escorting us as we glide down a shimmering fairway towards the sun. After they move on, I return to my cockpit cushion, relieved of the wheel by the windvane. I stretch and yawn, and snuggle into its warmth.

'Does it get any better than this?' Barbara asks dreamily, fluffing up the pillow under her head.

'Guess we'll have to go there to find out.'

• • • • •

BEAUFORT IS ALREADY IN THE SIXTIES when we finally start moving the next morning. We trade our blue jeans for shorts. It feels like the beginning of the rest of the trip.

We phone Kirsten. She and the girls will arrive by bus in the early evening. We luxuriate in the sun, a beer and a bowl of soup on a balcony overlooking the river. We take a late afternoon stroll through streets that feel like the Old South.

We have sailed through fear to this warm place. We have conquered nothing: not uncertainty, surely not the sea. If anything, we are loosening our grip on the illusion of conquest, settling down into our all-too-evident frailty.

Perhaps it is enough to show up, to submit to the lessons the sea will undoubtedly give.

•••••

THE NEXT MONTH TAKES US DOWN the coasts of North Carolina, South Carolina and Georgia. Warm and mild weather mostly. The routine of boat school punctuated with thirty-hour excursions out into the Atlantic. Between passages we relax down into new places, and a cruising lifestyle that increasingly feels natural. In mid-December we set the second anchor in Fernandina Beach, Florida, scout up a cheap rental car, and drive North for the Christmas holidays with our families.

Christmas is still settling in my midsection when Dan, David and I embark on an irreverence-laced drive back to Florida. Barbara and the girls will linger in Michigan, meeting me in Miami when her father drives down after the New Year.

We deal in a familiar blend of catching up and derision during two raucous days on the road. At some point I admit to the sense of foreboding that dogs me, an apparent residue of the cardiac wars. I resent the fact that it is still there all these miles later.

'What'd you expect, John – that you'd just skate through all of that untouched?' David chuckles, mocking my insolence.

'You've always been a bit of a wuss,' Dan reminds us. 'So what's new?'

We laugh. The dread does not go away.

I am relieved to find *Grace* anchored where we left her, in the centre of the tide-ridden Saint Mary's River. On the morning we left for Michigan we woke to find her almost a quarter of a mile up the river. Her anchor had dragged during the night. The nightmare of having her vanish infected my holidays.

We wait impatiently for two windswept days. Twenty-five-knot Northerlies bear with them the coldest Florida weather anyone can remember. A weather window swings open midweek, with weakening Northerlies for the next couple of days.

Buoyed by the forecast and the already moderating winds, we set sail at dusk for Palm Beach, two hundred and forty miles to the South. The next forty hours are uneventful, the variable Northerlies clocking to the East by New Year's Day. The wind picks up in the afternoon, an almost warm fifteen knots on the beam. David affixes himself to a radio and makes regular reports on the bowl games. We are making the best time of our passage.

'Palm Beach by midnight,' I proclaim. Nothing in the weather report or on the horizon seems contrary.

In the late afternoon, however, clouds begin piling up in the East, grey at first, then going black. I pull on foul-weather gear in anticipation of a dowsing. Bank after bank of clouds fly through, but very little in the way of rain.

'False alarm?' Dan asks, climbing up into the cockpit.

The clouds continue to charge up over the horizon, dark and ominous now, extinguishing the sun to the West. A few crooked fingers reach above them, probing the New Year's sky. To play it safe, we shorten sails in the early evening.

'Should make for an easier ride in these swells.' Big swells and growing.

'Where are they coming from?' Dan asks, to nobody in particular.

The evening answers with yet another acceleration, a steady twenty knots now, seas to match. We shorten sails again.

'No sense beating our brains out.'

'Done enough damage already.'

Midnight closes in with yet another escalation. We douse what is left of the genoa. The seas are pounding at us now, body blows against *Grace*'s hull, reaching through the lifelines to grab at us.

'I'll need some sighting help. I don't want to get in near that shore until we can see the channel.'

As we come up on Singer Island, just North of the Palm Beach inlet, none of us can see a channel marker in the maze of shore lights and breakers. I turn the engine on and ease in closer, a hedge against getting caught sideways in the increasingly confused seas.

By 12.45am, the GPS assures us that we are at the latitude of the inlet. We still can't see the channel through the turbulence ahead. Squalls are rolling through now, one after another, further obscuring the channel lights we know are out there.

'A real mess.'

'And getting worse,' from Dan, not known for flinching in bad weather. It begins to rain.

A rogue wave crashes over the transom and into the cockpit, tossing me up against the wheel. A dagger thrust to the chest, the searing memory of scar tissue stretched beyond the familiar.

'I don't like it, but we have to go in closer. We'll never pick up those channel markers otherwise.'

Grace is holding her own, in spite of the pounding we

are taking. I don't want to get too near to the shore, vulnerable to a loss of sail or power. We weave back and forth across the heaving confusion of wave crests and shore lights where we believe we will find the inlet. We can't make it out. The ocean is in open revolt now, wildly gyrating seascape backdropped by an anarchy of lights.

'I know it's there, John, but for the life of me, I can't see it.'

The engine alarm comes on without warning. I drop to a knee to check the barely visible gauges. The oil pressure has dropped to zero. After several failed attempts to restart it, I click off the ignition.

'It's gone, Dan. I don't think we'll get it going in these conditions.'

It has probably sucked air up into the diesel line, or oil dislodged from the bottom of a fuel tank.

'Damn,' the first stab of fear. 'Let's try to take her back out.'

I swing *Grace* back towards the swells. They are riding each other to alarming proportions now, occasionally breaking.

Dan sheets in the main, tries to buy us momentum to face the onslaught. *Grace* lurches forward, shuddering when she's hit, then wallowing on. I have never seen so many squalls, storms within a storm, one after another, unrelenting. *We are going to run you aground, grind you to bits.*

By 2am, we are just holding our own in the war that is sweeping over us. We may not be making headway, but neither are we losing ground. I concentrate on keeping our bow from dipping into the breaking waves. Most of the time it works. An occasional rogue rides another wave over us, crashing down the length of the deck, over the cabin top and into the cockpit.

'Nothing I can do.'

Every time we get pooped, we shake ourselves off, look at each other, and laugh in amazement.

'Nice little New Year's sail,' I shout to David.

'A regular walk in the park.'

Our walk in the park ends abruptly when the main tears apart, the casualty of an unseen wall of wind that sweeps me off the wheel, over a hatch, and into the back-stay. I pull myself back to the helm, drenched in pain and disbelief.

'This is trouble.'

For the moment, there is nothing we can do but save what's left of the main. Dan moves quickly to the mast, hanging on as a breaking wave tries to take his feet out from under him. He drags down the flagging remnants, lashing them to the boom. I stand at the helm, continuing to work the wheel as if it mattered. We have no speed, no leverage, no control over where *Grace* goes. Nothing to protect her from swells that are now pounding us broad-side, all knees and elbows, mounting the hull and clam-bering over the deck, rolling us chaotically as they pass through.

It has us now, the storm and the beckoning shore.

We are contacted on the radio by a tug boat captain, intent on helping us decipher the channel markers. He alerts the Coast Guard somehow. 'Their local communica-tion tower just blew away,' he reports. They are in contact with us in minutes, patching transmissions through the tower at Miami.

I answer their questions numbly, shouting to be heard. I am pitching about the cabin, trying not to yank the microphone off the face of the radio. I am getting very sick.

Yes, the sails are out of play. 'I don't think I can keep us off the shore with a foresail.'

And the engine is down. 'I don't think we can get it going in these conditions. Or *keep* it going if we could restart it.'

Yes, we could use a tow. 'If you've got anything that can get to us.' It feels like an admission of defeat, a concession statement. I am too sick to care. Dan steps in, GPS in hand, and gives them our position.

'We are still a good way from shore.'

I lurch back to the cockpit, profoundly seasick for the first time in ten years, my energy vanished. I struggle to stay oriented. Being outside helps, the wind and the now horizontal rain and spray, the sheer fury of it a distraction.

'They're on their way,' Dan returns to the cockpit. 'Should take them at least an hour.'

'If we've got that long,' trying not to retch.

All hell is breaking loose now, one squall after another washing over us with winds so strong that the rain is lethal. The world is flying by with freight train intensity, the wind veering when you think you've got your back to it, forcing your face down into your hands. Gusts tear violently at anything that dares to stand. The rigging shrieks like a herd of wounded animals. I jam my boots into the corner of the settee across from me, and reach back to hold the lifeline behind me. I try to shelter my face with the other hand. Dan and David are doing the same thing.

'You okay?'

'Great. You?'

'Terrific.'

The squalls are bad but strangely tolerable. The same blistering wind that bowls us over on our side also pins us there. We have a bizarre, suspended stability. Sustained gusts flatten the onrushing waves with their velocity and the leaden downpour they contain. We are rocked and thrown, rocked and thrown again, but mostly in a stable, laid-over position.

When a squall moves on and the wind drops, we are left with the overpowering height and weight of the resurrected swells. There is nothing to steady or protect us. Great slabs of saltwater rock us unmercifully, arch up over us, pounce when they get us sideways. *We can take you any time we want.* We are thrown wildly from side to side, unable to steady ourselves. I am amazed that *Grace* doesn't roll on over. She somehow keeps her gyrating mast out of the water.

I lift my eyes long enough to take a bead on land. The Gulf Stream is rapidly taking us North, maybe helping us to stay offshore. If we do wash in now, it will probably be on a beach.

Mostly, I'm just trying to avoid getting sicker. Nothing I do, not deep breathing or distraction, or staying as motionless as possible, seems to help. I remind myself I've been seasick before. It is thin reassurance.

There are other voices now, murmuring within. A low-grade ache in my chest that grows with every lost degree of body temperature. A mounting concern that this beating, nausea, and the deepening chill will take me beyond the normal pain, into the zone where the heart explodes.

Breathe.

'Here they come!' David announces. Lights flicker on the horizon, blue flashes over the lace-curtain tips of the swells. I can see them directly now, closing, strobe light eruptions in the maelstrom. A chunky bulldog of a boat punches through a receding wall of rain. She circles us tentatively, her diesel roar just audible within that other unrelenting din.

'Let me do this,' Dan shouts and he's up at the bow, catching a lead line on the second throw. He drops to his knees to secure it on our Samson post, then crawls back to the cockpit. The Coast Guard boat is moving away now, its crew playing out a towline the length of a football field. It catches as they disappear behind the swells, springs to attention through a crest. We jerk forward a bit, and settle in. We are moving.

The sea is releasing its prisoners. This time.

Dan offers to take the wheel. I yield the helm with nothing more than a nauseous 'thank you'. He is covering for me once again.

We are underway, with motion that feels like safety. Only a tow to the channel. I slide down the companionway and sprawl on a berth, hanging on, pulling a sleeping bag over me. I need to break this chill.

A series of lightning storms escorts us as we make a wide, wave-tossed arc, first to the Southeast, into the swells and deeper water. Later we angle back towards the channel to the West. Dan is astride a bucking bronco, tethered, barely in control. Occasionally he shouts his amazement, or is it fear?

'Ride 'em, cowboy!'

He shouts down to me as we make our final approach, and asks me to take the helm to navigate the swell-ravaged channel entrance. Perhaps he is trying to shore up my confidence. The icy wheel is a shock to my warming hands.

Dawn is breaking when we finally reach an anchorage next to Peanut Island. It seems fitting. Excitement and relief are shouted back and forth to the weary Coast Guard crew.

'The worst I've ever seen,' one of them exhales.

'I thought we were going over. *Twice*!' the flushed, young skipper admits.

'It had us,' I tell him. 'You took us back. Risked yourselves to do it. Thank you.'

The winds are dropping quickly now. It is almost still by the time we set the anchor. The morning sky is an understated rose, the wildlife shocked to silence in the mangroves. The storm is over.

We slouch into formless heaps around the deck, quiet for a long while. There will be time later for comparing notes, acting out the excited decompression that always follows a great storm. For now there are clothes to strip off, a great shattered main to bundle up, and bunks into which to collapse.

But not without some parting shots.

'Thanks, John, for the Florida cruise.'

'I can't wait to get back home.'

•••••

'It says we got thirty-one inches of rain in nine hours.' I am talking to Barbara from a roadside phone booth, the Palm Beach Post propped in front of me.

The headline story describes a rare 'train echo' storm spawned when two distinct fronts collided over us, touching off a line of thunderstorms 'like box cars on a train'. At least one tornado was involved, and tornadic winds 'up to 112 miles per hour.' The storm snapped concrete power poles, tossed cargo containers, flipped tractor trailers, ripped roofs from homes, and toppled portable classrooms.

'These rascals are pretty rare, it says, almost impossible to predict. The national weather guy is quoted as saying, "The whole area blew up."'

'I don't know how strong those winds were. *Blowing up* sounds right.'

'I'm just happy you are okay,' Barbara has a quake in her voice.

'We're fine, and *Grace* is too. The sail may be a goner, but the engine should be easy to fix.'

Barbara has gone very quiet.

'We were lucky. We got trounced, and I wasn't worth a damn after I got sick.'

'What is that about?'

'I don't know. I had a patch on, too.' I have used medicinal patches behind my ear for a decade now, whenever there is heavy weather. I have never been ill when using it.

'Maybe it's affected by all the other medication I take.' I add what we both know. 'I can't be getting sick out there.'

'That's for sure,' is all she says, unwilling to pile it on.

'And your heart?'

'Not too bad. The cold bothered me most of all.'

Again, Barbara is silent. I want to shift gears.

'This was *not* a piece of cake.' It doesn't sound as funny out loud.

•••••

DAVID LEAVES TO GET BACK TO WORK. Dan and I motor down the intracoastal waterway to his departure from Lauderdale.

'Give me a call any time you want extra crew. But I want to *sail* next time. No more of these candy-ass day trips!'

We sift through the debris, looking for lessons, mostly what we already know: always anticipate an engine breakdown, a torn sail, or both; stay off those lee shores; get a storm trysail ready, one that you can get up in extreme conditions.

'And don't get sick,' I add.

I can laugh, but my confidence has taken another hit. *Am I up to this?*

Like it or not, I am different from the man who single-handed the Atlantic ten years ago. Wiser, maybe, perhaps even better. But not stronger, not healthier. I don't have the physical brashness I took to sea then, or into daily life just two years ago.

I have lost one of the three arteries that keep my heart alive. I've lost something else, that animal certainty that I will prevail, no matter what.

Will my heart fail me in a tight spot? After all these miles, I'm still not sure.

I leave in the morning. Dan tosses me the docklines with a terse, 'have a good sail'. I angle *Grace* out into the tidal current that will take me down the channel. Three miles and I'll be back in the open Atlantic. This time I am alone.

A mild Westerly fills the slackened sails when I clear the pierhead. It asks nothing more than attention to the helm. Last night's chill has blown out to obliteration in the Bahamas. I relax down into the late-morning sun.

Grace and I begin a long arc to the South. The storm at Palm Beach rides along, old film already, black and white. Maybe the wind will go out of it if it plays long enough. Maybe it will sit down quietly in the hall of memory: sit down and shut up.

•••••

WE ARE DEEP INTO JANUARY NOW, enjoying the luxury of Miami Beach Marina. John Ryan and his girlfriend, Darcy, join us there, as do a series of friends.

Tony Mance and I have known each other since graduate school. The product of a Mississippi River steel town, he is a furnace in his own right. Beneath the craggy Croatian exterior, the barrage of deeply held beliefs, he has an uncommon sweetness and a very linear loyalty. Tony would cover your back in the darkest of alleys, or die trying.

We spend long hours catching up, ogling the diverse beauty of South Beach.

'So what do you do all day?' Tony has not stepped back from his day job yet.

'I write when we're not underway, usually until late afternoon.'

'I love the stories you've shown me, John. But you don't have to go out there and get beaten up to write. You could do that here, today, sitting at this table.' Tony has never been very happy about my sailing with a gimpy heart.

'I could, but it wouldn't be the same. Burroughs talks

about immersing yourself in the life you want to write about, *submitting* – his word – to conditions you may not have bargained for.'

'Palm Beach?'

'I sure as hell wasn't looking for it. It came looking for us. Had some questions to ask.'

'Questions?'

'Lots of them. Do we control the big stuff? Do we *have* to? Will life give us what we need? Not necessarily what we *think* we need, or exactly what we want . . .'

He looks on impassively.

'I'm a slow learner, Tony. I have to be reminded – over and over again – to stop trying to *make* everything happen.'

When he says nothing, I add, 'I do like what happens when I slow down, maybe *do* less and *experience* more.'

'I've been telling you that for thirty years,' Tony erupts, wiping saliva from his lips. He throws his napkin down, leans in towards me. 'You finally listening?' He reaches across and slaps my face playfully, a mock wake-up call. We lean back and laugh, say nothing for a while, looking out to sea.

'Maybe good writing and a rich life have that in common, Tony: radical attention, moments really experienced . . .'

'More of that Zen gibberish, John?'

I'm not biting.

'. . . The aroma of this cup of coffee, Tony, what the sun does to the tablecloth. The fine curve of that woman's forearm.'

Tony is off balance for a moment, the 'forearm' I think.

'It's a kind of prayer . . .'

'Damnit, John,' Tony cuts me off, swiping at the table cloth, overflowing with exasperation. 'Where do you get this crap?' He looks down with barely controlled agitation, then sideways, back out to sea. The waitress arrives in the nick of time.

He pays the bill, leaving her a hefty tip.

'Gotta take care of my unemployed friends,' he tells her, pushing away my extended twenty.

We don't talk much on the way back, the silence of old friends. We enter the marina, the almost saffron scent of the shrubbery.

'Hey, John . . .'

'Yeah?'

'I'm not going to tell you what to do . . .' *Here it comes.* 'But I'd think about getting back on the meds.'

•••••

JOHN AND RHONDA LISKEY are a throwback to Bonnie and Clyde. Three children and 25 years have nudged them in the direction of good citizenship. They were designed, however, with the cross-country road trip in mind: a dated convertible, the music up high. They have come to Miami to see us.

'Don't you worry about the girls – how high they can climb on the rigging?' Rhonda and John have two girls of their own, older than Katie and Erin.

'Good exercise,' I reply nonchalantly, pretending to live out beyond my fears. 'They're not strong enough to go up far.'

Later in the week I glance out an opening port to see a cluster of people on the dock, looking up. One is pulling out a camera.

When I step up into the cockpit, Katie takes pre-emptive action.

'Hi, Dad.'

I look up and shudder. Katie and Erin are standing casually on the first set of spreaders, twenty feet above the deck, one hand for the shroud, the other for the mast.

The trust exercises you don't go looking for. They are smiling down, clearly full of themselves.

Uncharacteristically stopping to think before I speak – *they are strong enough to get up there* – I take a deep breath.

'Good for you,' I pass the first test.

'Don't go any higher,' I cannot restrain myself. '*Please* be careful.'

We all need a little room, room and some time in the sun.

I nod at their admirers and retreat below. Better not to see sometimes.

●●●●●

A SECOND, DEEPER LAYER OF WEARINESS gets exposed during the interlude at South Beach. There are mornings when neither of us wakes up until 10am, the kids' voices ricocheting down from the cockpit.

'As I relax, I feel more tired than ever,' Barbara admits.

'Two years in the pressure cooker, you've earned it.'

'Maybe we ought to slow it all down, just rest up.'

'What do you have in mind?' I am wary.

'I don't know. It might make sense to hang out in the Keys for a couple of months, instead of sprinting down to Panama and through the canal.'

It makes more sense than I want to admit. I am afraid of losing momentum, as if I can outrun fate.

'It's hard to think of changing plans . . .' I am rubbing the seams in my forehead. 'We might get too comfortable, or too timid.'

'Most people wouldn't think what we're doing is particularly timid,' Barbara has an edge in her voice.

'No, but there's this whole new sense of being at risk somehow . . .'

'You *are* at risk, John.' Barbara looks as if she wants to take the words back as soon as she says them. She plunges on.

'So maybe you shouldn't be too hard on yourself. You are always talking about how people come by their feelings honestly. How about you? You got the billy-hell shaken right out of you.'

She has caught me again. It is a special arrogance to deny yourself the breathing room you give to others.

'But that only applies to mortals.'

She absolves me with a smile.

'So maybe we ought to slow it down another notch, more than catch our breath.'

'Tear up the plan?' I ask with mock horror.

'What was it John Lennon said about planning?' She invites concession.

•••••

WE SAUNTER DOWN THE KEYS in February, and anchor in Boot Key at Marathon. We settle into a rhythm of boat school and writing and long languid interludes on the beach. Sand in your swimsuit, life in slow motion.

During a lazy afternoon's read, I stumble onto a gentle admonition from the Tao: 'As to family life, be totally present.' I read it to Barbara.

'Sounds like what we're doing, John.'

It seems inconceivable that we will ever regret this lapse from the urgency we have called living.

•••••

MARCH IS RUNNING DOWN NOW. April is on her way, and – beyond that – hurricane season. What are we going to do?

On those infrequent days when squalls roll in, I stand on the deck, or sit there, looking for answers in my reaction to the wind.

My uncertainty intensifies after a serious bout of vertigo. I suddenly feel lightheaded while browsing in a local bookshop. I reach for the edge of a table to steady myself. I feel like vomiting. I lurch through the aisles and out the door, bruising my shoulder as I miss the opening. I collapse down on a bench outside, unable to sit up, much less stand. Is this my heart, a stroke, food poisoning? I don't know, and I can't do anything about it anyway. I close my eyes and pretend to be napping, embarrassed at my sorry state.

'John, is that you?'

I'm not focusing very well, but I'd know Frank's voice anywhere. I last saw him in Fernandina Beach, months ago. I try to explain, cutting him off when he mentions the hospital.

'Could you please just take our dinghy – it's on the dock across the parking lot – and get Barbara. *Grace* is just off the main channel.'

Frank is back with Barbara in minutes. After a brief discussion they lead me towards the dinghy dock, supporting me on either side.

'I just want to get to the boat.'

They ease me down into the dinghy. I vomit over the side as we motor away.

I spend the rest of the day clinging to a cockpit seat, trying to stay motionless. Any movement, even the slightest, has the world spinning again, nausea washing over me.

'If there's anything I need out there, it's my balance.'

'Let's not worry about *out there*,' Barbara remains lucid. 'One step at a time.'

I slip into an uneasy sleep as night closes in. I wake up to vertigo and despair, then drift off again.

I feel a little better by morning. I move tentatively around the boat. I try some breakfast. Any sudden movement sends me spinning again. By evening I am more steady. I am only slightly dizzy by dawn the next day.

My head clears in coming days. It takes several weeks to feel entirely normal. By that time, I have talked to Rick.

'Sounds like labrynthitis to me. It's a weird kind of virus. Just went away?'

'Just went away.'

* * * * *

THE GIRLS DO BETTER THAN DISTRACT.

Six-year old Erin, the family philosopher, draws on fortune-cookie wisdom every time a discussion of plans elicits even a furled brow.

'Dad, the journey is the destination.'

'Where did you get that?'

'I don't know,' she answers coyly. 'Maybe I just thought it up.'

'Good thinking, kiddo.'

Katie, who combines hard-edge realism with a practical desire to fix whatever needs fixing, has amassed over one hundred dollars, birthday cash supplementing her scrupulously saved weekly allowance.

'I've decided to donate a hundred dollars to the Save-a-Turtle Fund.'

'What's that?'

'It's a foundation to save the loggerhead sea turtles.'

'Are you sure?' I try to talk her down to a smaller donation '. . . so you have some to spend on yourself.'

'The sea turtles need it more than I do, Dad.'

• • • • •

A MAGAZINE EDITOR GETS INTO THE MIX, contacting me about a story I have submitted.

'We love your work, John. But we've got lots of stories about families and children, more than we need. What makes your story unique is your heart: how you have survived, first of all, then gone to sea.'

I am surprised by the intensity of my reaction. I try to respond evenly.

'To tell the story without my family is to miss the real story. I am alive *because* of them.'

'It's not personal,' Barbara points out later. 'They know their market. They just want stories slanted to their readers.'

She's right, I know. But I have difficulty letting go.

• • • • •

It's 3AM, but we need to talk.

'How do you *really* feel, Barbara?'

Barbara blinks her way awake. She rubs her eyes. She inspects the clock in a state of disbelief. She looks at me, bristles slightly, and exhales.

'. . . About being woken up at three in the morning?'

'Not about that. About going across.'

'Jeez, John,' she exhales again. She doesn't say anything for a moment, closing her eyes and breathing deeply.

'Don't tell me what you think I want to hear. I want to know how you feel, reservations and all.'

Barbara purses her lips, but doesn't remind me not to patronize her.

'Okay, let's start with my reservations, get them out of the way.

'The Atlantic is not the Caribbean, fifteen steady knots and a sunny eighty degrees. The North Atlantic, in May, is everything from becalmed to impossible. I'm not crazy about getting beaten up, especially with the kids aboard. And we *will* get beaten up some of the time.'

'I understand. What else?'

'You're not sure about the windvane. I really don't want to hand-steer all the way, trying to do boat school in the off hours.'

'I agree. What else?'

Long pause, too long, 'My heart?'

'We still don't know what you can handle, do we?'

'No, we don't.' I don't want to interrupt her list. 'What else?'

'Those are my biggest reservations,' looking directly at me now, 'but I can feel your engine revving up. You'd rather go to Ireland than to New England.' She is up on an elbow, chin cupped in her hand.

'Your turn.'

'I don't want to get hammered either, especially with the girls. I wouldn't even consider it if I thought they'd be traumatized or endangered. I think they'll respond to how *we* respond, more than to the ocean itself. And we'll handle whatever gets dished out.'

'Think so?'

'It won't always be pretty, but we'll hold it together – *because* the girls are with us.'

Barbara says nothing.

'The windvane should work when we shift weight to the stern, get the boat better balanced.'

Now for the hard part.

'My heart is the question mark. The Atlantic will be a test. I wouldn't consider going out there if I didn't think I could handle it . . . and if I didn't believe you could get *Grace* home without me.'

Barbara rolls her eyes in exasperation. 'Which is it, John: I can sail her home *or* your heart is strong enough to do it?'

'Both.' Don't take the bait. 'The only way we will *know* is by going.'

'Touché,' she looks down, smirks, then back.

'So what would you like to do, Irish?'

'It must be beautiful there in July.'

We both break into wide smiles, smiles that seal the deal.

●●●●●

We sail back to Fort Lauderdale in mid-April, mooring *Grace* just south of the bridge at Las Olas. We take a flight back to Michigan to spend some time with John Ryan and our parents. When we return to Lauderdale, the clock is running.

We work frantically to get *Grace* ready. Katie and Erin join in. Because they are not teenagers yet, they still like us. Because they don't know they are not supposed to like mechanical things, they seem to genuinely enjoy getting their knuckles skinned on projects around the boat.

There is plenty to do. Provisions of food and medicine compete with sailing equipment, tools and spare parts for limited storage space. The girls pare their toys down to a treasured few, even as I begrudgingly leave some books behind. The boat is a jumbled mess for several days, adding to pre-departure tension. When things are about to boil over, we take late afternoon breaks on the beach. In the evenings we decompress with walks down Las Olas to the bookstore and coffee shops. The ice cream parlour becomes a regular stop.

On a couple of occasions, Barbara and I bargain with the girls for a morning 'date' alone. We rise early and row to shore. Over breakfast on a veranda looking out at the ocean, we monitor each other's resolve.

'Do you really think we can sail her across?' Barbara is watching the procession of rollers from the Northeast.

'We don't have to,' I quip. She looks up, puzzled.

'*Grace* will sail herself across. We just have to help her.'

●●●●●

AFTER A WEEK OF BOISTEROUS NORTHERLIES, we get our chance. A weather window opens, forty-eight hours to clear the Gulf Stream and the Great Bahama Shoals. Late in the afternoon we round the pierhead at Fort Lauderdale, swing North into the Atlantic. Brusque Southeasterlies greet us, rolling *Grace* awkwardly in the swells. Barbara and I glance at each other, equal parts anxiety and determination.

'Here we go.'

'Again.'

Our passage plan is simple enough: north to twenty-eight degrees latitude, then a rhumbline to Bermuda. We later take a more southerly track when a series of lows converge north of us, raining mayhem on sailors caught in the area.

The windvane decides to work, relieving us of the need to be at the wheel every second. We know in advance that the crossing will be physically draining. We work at pacing ourselves, build a schedule and mostly stick with it.

I do longer watches than Barbara. She more than compensates with meal preparation and attention to the girls. We squeeze in naps whenever we can. At night we use an egg-timer to ensure regular scans of the horizon. This is especially important near the shipping lanes, where freighters come up on you quickly.

By the third day we are slipping into a comfortable rhythm. We gradually adjust to the three-dimensional pitch, roll and yawl that play havoc with internal chemistry. The girls quickly adapt to our new routine. They recognize when we are getting tired, and entertain themselves when one of us sleeps. Katie settles into long periods of reading in the cockpit. We let them do an occasional daytime watch in mild weather. We relish the luxury of two-hour naps together.

After dinner each evening, I take a six-hour watch. The commotion below quickly settles. Lights go off for good when Barbara turns in. She needs to bank some sleep for her long, early morning watch.

I am left with the fading light in the West, the saltwater aroma, the lush roll of the boat. A late spring moon arrives unannounced, calling me out beyond thought. Boundaries blur – that familiar sense of separateness – then give way altogether. For a while there is only *Grace*, the waves, and the seamless breeze. A sky also, in which only the brightest star can compete with the rising moon.

•••••

AFTER FOUR DAYS OF EASY NORTHWESTERLIES, our initiation is over. The first sustained thunderstorms roll in on increasingly raucous winds, jagged flashes in an ever-changing sky.

During the day they are strenuous enough. 'Shall we reef now?'

With darkness they assert complete dominance, inviting you to kneel. You see them coming, sometimes for an hour before they arrive. Time enough to contract down into a hard corner of yourself. You zig and zag, play hide-and-seek with them. You may escape for a while, but they will catch you in the end.

Another lightshow flickers on the horizon. 'Close the hatches.' That long march down towards us, arc announcing clap at shorter and shorter intervals. The bolts themselves, thick as trees, explode and sizzle, incandescent. *Try to bridge heaven and earth*, they shout. *Try*.

I am too enthralled to anticipate the wall of wind that bends us over. The sails and shrouds are shrieking now, *Grace* bolting like a fugitive colt, hurdling the suddenly aroused swells. There is nowhere to hide. I lift my hands from the wheel, an illusion that I can protect myself.

They'll pass, I remind myself, like fits of rage. Analysis doesn't help when they close in, the hand across my eyes a hapless, florid x-ray. I am intoxicated by the ozone in the air.

It is only when they have trundled on, a relentless quest of this horizon and the next, that I relax down into their splendour: beauty that has passed by, as it often does, sucking out my breath.

•••••

NINE DAYS OUT, Barbara sights the first light at Bermuda. It is 1am. We glide into the cut at St Georges Harbour by mid-morning. We anchor in a cluster of boats a quarter of a mile off the Custom-House quay.

The girls lead us in an unembarrassed 'three cheers for us', for our first thousand-mile passage on *Grace*. It is a celebration that will continue for the better part of a week.

We go ashore for long periods, basking in the easy warmth of Bermuda. We share tables and trade tales with sailors from all over the world. We meet at quayside bars and cockpit gatherings, potlucks and fish fries that spring up spontaneously. Everyone has a story to tell, often coaxed into the open after a beer or two.

We indulge the unique camaraderie of those who have

sailed long distances, veterans of those lesser wars, the instant intimacy of those just off the saltwater plain, blinking at that other, shoreside world. Whether you arrive on a sixty-foot Swan or a homemade, ferro-cement special, you have crossed the same watery wilderness and muddled through the same harsh nights and days. Whatever our differences, we are welded together by a common willingness to offer ourselves up to the sea.

Katie and Erin link up immediately with two girls off an English boat, and another off a Belgian. They are inseparable for the duration of our stay, enjoying dinghy rides, swimming and giggling in the park. We operate with loose schedules, designed to accommodate their play. Every bedtime is too early, dawn not soon enough.

The girls flaunt their own version of saltwater pride, their respect for other 'cruising kids'. When anyone moves on, addresses are shared and radio contacts arranged. Their relationships, instant and unencumbered, are compressed by the limits of available time.

Our gypsy lifestyle asks a lot of them. They seem to be adjusting well, thriving. Their obvious happiness makes it hard to dwell on the concerns we brought out onto the Atlantic.

This next leg – 1,900 miles to the Azores – will tell.

• • • • •

'It was terrible,' she blurts. Her dishevelled husband looks on, nodding.

'What makes it hard,' he whispers aside, 'is that we've planned and saved so long.'

We are sitting at a dockside cafe, watching a nearby

cruise ship disgorge. Our new acquaintances are part of the bedraggled army straggling down the gangplank. They plop in the first chairs they can find. In their sixties probably, they are every bit as exhausted as the arriving sailors, with little of the surging sense of accomplishment.

They have their own story to tell: departure from the East Coast, nausea deepening with every intensification of the weather. Then, at the mouth of the harbour, a day-long hesitation, waiting for the swells to subside. A hospital ship now, even an occasional, uniformed crew member bent over the rail, retching into the sea. The cruise from hell.

We talk long enough for their stomachs to settle. They order a pizza tentatively: 'hold the anchovies, please'. Their spirits lift, colour ebbing slowly into the ashen portions of their faces. The husband springs back first, entranced by our family's adventure. He is warm and generous, not a twinge of envy in his excited questions.

'Don't you get scared?' she is looking directly at Barbara.

'I'd be afraid!' She looks at the girls now, marshalling support.

'Courage only happens when you are afraid,' Katie chimes in, uninvited.

'. . . Not letting fear run your life,' Erin adds, in what has become a dinner table mantra.

I look on in uncharacteristic silence. Brave talk, and easy. Now for the hard part.

•••••

'WE'VE GOT OUR WEATHER WINDOW,' a fellow sailor intones over the VHF. 'We'll be leaving within the hour.'

'Us, too,' Barbara says, glancing over to where I nod agreement. 'Later this afternoon.'

We dilute our anxiety with a flurry of battening down and storing away. We have slept in, gorged ourselves on shore food, regaled and been regaled by new friends and old. We have taken on fresh provisions, and made the most necessary repairs. A weather window seems to be opening, its importance underlined by a dismasted boat that limps back into St Georges, an emergency signal that is activated in a storm a hundred miles north. You take what is given, and don't overreach.

Whatever hesitations we have, it is time to go.

•••••

THE FIRST WEEK MAKES A MOCKERY of the forecast for fair winds. A series of squalls march through, punctuating otherwise light winds and lulls. We languish becalmed when we are not getting our brains beaten out.

'Is it something I said?' to the stolid sky, which does not deign to answer. Seven days out, we have four days' miles to show. Radio acquaintances, staying safely south, are not faring much better. Though everyone tries to stay upbeat in their daily contacts, the weather is getting on our nerves, wearing us down.

The crew of *Grace* hangs in there. Barbara keeps us well fed, regardless of conditions. Boat school goes on. Classes are short, requiring more effort than usual. A despised combination of windless days and swells, the residue of distant storms, takes its toll. When there is wind, it comes in dense, squallish proportions, often out of the East.

'Didn't anybody tell them about pilot charts?' I complain to Barbara. Years of accumulated weather wisdom prescribe dominant Southwesterlies.

We try to make the most of what we've got, angling further to the North. We talk with the girls about the toughness it takes to sail the Atlantic. Between the lines, we are talking to ourselves, grappling with that 'what-in-hell-are-we-doing-out-here?' sense that seeps into foul-weather passages.

Sometimes I have answers. Sometimes, especially during squalls, I can only stand at the helm, an ache in my chest, dumbstruck at the raw power of it, the beauty within the uproar. The rolling, blowing pod of passing pilot whales pulls me out beyond everything I call normal, beyond the confines of self, and into that larger life, so suddenly available. The horizon, broad enough for both ends of an arching rainbow. The undulating, pulsating seascape, up and down and across, on which *Grace* somehow muscles forwards.

I am drenched again in ocean reality, the way it undermines whatever frail sense of certainty you bring out here. The staysail that unlocks a forestay shackle, and flies out over the lifelines in the howling 3m. The mischievous windvane that works free of the boat's transom and threatens to abandon ship altogether. How the wind chafes sheets and halyards to their breaking point, and you to your breaking point – the burgeoning sense that who you are is more – and the saltwater gnaws at everyone and everything.

'Amazing,' I mutter through an afternoon without margin.

Amazing, too, what ocean air does to an appetite, to a

hot plate of food. How the mystery of a boat's motion alchemizes land-based chemistry, yielding dreams as vivid as the evening stars. What a persistent storm does, how it strips away every accessory, leaving you round-shouldered, sentient, primitive.

The wind begins backing around to the Northwest, intensifying as it goes.

'Finally,' Barbara sputters when she takes the helm for the graveyard watch. By morning we are hurdling along to the East, exhilarated by our progress. Exhilaration yields to alarm as the wind keeps building. We take in a reef as *Grace* continues to accelerate.

'Maybe we ought to take in another,' Barbara cautions at noon. By mid-afternoon we are double-reefed. An hour later we replace the partially furled genoa with a small staysail.

'That's better, isn't it?' We are riding more comfortably now, Barbara's sea-sense in play.

'Those are some serious swells.' She stands in the companionway, squinting, then retreats below to work with the girls.

It is no accident that I have never replaced the broken wind speed or hull speed indicators. I move fast enough on land. Barbara resorts to a hand-held wind indicator and the GPS. I prefer to feel the wind, sense our boat speed. It calls me out of my head and into my body. I adjust sails as necessary.

'Never early enough,' Barbara mutters, the weight of history in support.

'Nine point eight knots!' Katie shouts up over the companionway slat, GPS in hand.

'Isn't that *too* fast?' Barbara asks, concern in her eyes.

'It's pretty fast, but *Grace* is under control.' After days of inconsistent wind, speed feels good.

Struggling with tangled sheets later, I sense that 'bubbly' feeling in the centre of my chest, first described to a cardiologist several years ago. It happens when my heart is beating irregularly. It's disquieting to feel it out here. Nobody is asking.

It doesn't help that we are within days of the second anniversary of my open-heart surgery. I contract around the memory of it, huddle in self-absorption.

'Count your blessings,' I remind myself. Discomfort is a small price to pay for this extravagant bronco ride, the garlic-seasoned pasta Barbara is preparing below.

All any of us has is what we have right now.

●●●●●

RAIN SQUALLS CHASE US INTO THE NIGHT. It cools off quickly. The first deep chill of the passage calls up a swollen pain in my chest. I slide out a couple of companionway boards, easing myself down into the cabin.

'Got a low pushing in,' Barbara announces. The weather broadcast has just finished.

'Something else . . .' She's heating water for hot chocolate. 'Reports that a black-hulled seventy footer lost her keel and went over.'

'Where?' The knot in my chest tightens. The black-hulled boat of the girls' English friends is out here, days ahead of us.

'Long ways North of here, near the shipping lanes.' Barbara notices the look on my face, reaches out and touches my wrist.

'Their boat is nowhere near seventy feet,' she points out.

I nod, haunted by the pictures in my head. Nothing further is said, in order to keep from alarming the girls.

The squalls intensify through the night, robbing us of any deep sleep. Even though we are way out of position to be of help, I check and recheck the chart.

'Help will come out of the shipping lanes,' Barbara assures me. 'Freighters are probably there already.'

She's right, I know. I have a rancid stomach anyway.

The windvane calls me back to the here-and-now with its continuing effort to work free from the transom. I have regularly tightened the bolts that secure it. They cannot be snugged down any further. A design flaw allows them to cut into their nylon washers, making it impossible to get a wrench on them. I lash and relash the windvane frame to the transom, finally coming up with a rope harness I can cinch tight on a cockpit winch. It holds until dawn, when a new harness must be designed. The thought of hand-steering a thousand miles to the Azores inspires creativity and persistence.

In the morning, we hear that the crew of the capsized boat have been rescued.

'Amazing!' Barbara's voice is trembling with relief. 'Their keel just fell off, without much warning.'

•••••

CLOUDS PILE UP ON THE HORIZON late in the afternoon, omens of a pending assault. They close in around us, dampening the wind. Katie, with her natural sea-sense, sticks her head out of the companionway and inhales the overhanging calm. She scans the horizon and turns towards me.

'Do you think I should wake up Mom?'

'Not yet. Let her sleep.' I pull on foul-weather gear, still uncertain that this is the predicted low.

It's not the only thing I am unsure of.

For the first time in my life, I am not sure I can persist. Gone is the sense of physical invulnerability, donkey residue of a working-class childhood. Gone that perhaps irrational belief that I can take a beating and stay on my feet with sheer dint of will: run the marathon, complete the triathlon, sail across the ocean alone. In its place, clear as a graph on a hospital monitor, is the knowledge that this blood-starved heart has a limit, and at a certain point will go haywire. At what point?

I sit in the cockpit dressed for battle. The girls' voices ricochet up the companionway. Barbara is curled up asleep, hopefully on the face of a less ominous sea. The horizon surrenders to dark.

I can do this. I disengage the windvane and take hold of the wheel.

I can do this.

The calm deepens, still as a Sunday morning. The wind vanishes altogether, replaced by an eerie vacuum. The sails snap then droop, colts left outside before a great storm. Unnerved by their complaints, I switch on the engine, go in search of any breeze strong enough to give them some relief. Nothing works. The light ebbs out of the sky now. Barbara appears in the companionway.

'Weather?'

I nod, look up at the top of the mast for answers. The

derelict wind indicator gives up its whirling search, and settles in on the first stirrings of a Northwesterly. I switch off the engine.

Barbara soon returns to the cockpit in foul-weather gear. It is the hesitant beginning of a storm that builds through the night. We relieve each other regularly for naps we hope will take the edge off weariness. At dawn we shorten our sails, replacing the genoa with a small staysail.

Barbara glances at her watch as we change shifts.

'You're on your way now.'

It is 7am on 11th June, two years to the hour since the miracle workers at St Francis first wheeled me into the chilled confines of surgery. The wind is aroused and growling, under a now cloudless sky. The waves are in full eruption, row upon swelling row, an irregular assault by the towering rogue. All subtlety is slipping away: it's elbows and knees now, and icy fists against the hull.

The girls' eyes appear over the companionway slats, awakening to that wild gyration which is life below deck in weather like this. *Are we okay?*

'We're fine,' I shout above the commotion. I want to think that my smile reassures. Katie scribbles, 'I hate this day' on a pad of paper in her bunk.

I experiment with different angles of attack, at one point sailing directly downwind to rob the wind and swells of their throw-weight. Nothing seems to help.

'Pretty rough.' Barbara hands me a sealed mug of something hot. 'And we're pretty tired.' She argues lucidly for heaving to, long enough to get some rest.

'It's pretty difficult down below,' is enough.

Heaving to is something we've talked about a great

deal, but never attempted in conditions like these. Barbara doesn't remind me of the many times she suggested that we 'practise' it. We have a tense cockpit discussion of who does what. A sailing handbook is bandied about when we disagree, saltwater running down into its binding.

'Let's do it.'

I swing the bow through the wind to back the sails. *Grace* protests being bridled in, lunges, shudders, and stabilizes. The wind disarmed, our speed drops rapidly. *Grace* settles down, nudges forward, awkward but more comfortable. We are forty degrees off a wind that suddenly feels less ferocious.

'Isn't this better?' Barbara coaxes. 'We can get some rest.'

For several hours life borders on normal below deck: meals, naps, even an abbreviated attempt at boat school. I stay above mostly, alternating between cat naps hunched up behind the dodger and standing behind the wheel. It feels strange to be in heavy weather without wrestling the wheel. It takes a while to relax down into it, past the fear to appreciation for the sheer scale of the mayhem.

By late afternoon, the storm has vented much of its fury, weakening winds and seascape dramatics. We ease *Grace* out of suspended animation. She bolts to a gallop, headlong across the mountainous swells. Occasionally she dips her bow with exuberance, throws the top of a wave back down the length of the deck.

Still later, in the vivid hues of dusk, Barbara slips into the cockpit with a steaming thermos of soup. She scans the jagged horizon, glances down at her watch, then turns towards me.

'You're out of the first round of surgery now, in the recovery room.'

'I'll take the North Atlantic,' I grin back, as she retreats below to feed the girls.

No need to dwell on the low-grade ache that is back, to ride with me into the night.

•••••

THE TRANSITION TO SEA TIME RIPENS as the weather moderates. Days blend, one into another. Dates are lost altogether. Steady winds are standard fare, miles piling up behind us. We are nudged towards the illusion of ease.

Erin pops up into the cockpit one afternoon, a smile on her face. She is holding a folded paper.

'What's up, Erin?'

'Wrote a note to the ocean.'

'Good for you. Can I read it?'

'Sure, Dad,' and hands it to me.

Dear Ocean,

I just wanted to thank you for giving us such nice weather.

Love,
Erin

'Nice note, Erin.'

'Thanks, Dad.' She matter-of-factly drops it over the side, watches it bob in our wake for a while, then disappears below.

•••••

'IT'S GONE.' I LOOK UP out of the grimy engine compartment, and reach for a rag to wipe the grease off my hands.

The engine is down for good this time, seven hundred miles from the Azores. We have used it sparingly, low fuel and protests. It frequently stalls. It has been increasingly reluctant to start again.

'A fuel injector is shot. The starter too.' Looking for some good news, 'I can get the parts we need in the Azores.'

It is 4am, fresh evidence for the 'darkest hour'. We are hostages of the gorgeous calm that settled over us last night. The ocean stretches like a black waxed floor in every direction, under a moonlit sky. It is eerie and perfect, and – when the engine dies – profoundly still.

Barbara, exhausted, retreats to the cockpit for a long overdue cry.

'I know we're going to be okay,' anticipating my lame assurances. 'I'm just ready to be there. If the weather doesn't give us a break, it could take weeks.'

She's right. We are bone tired, juggling childcare, watches and sleep. Now this. A long way to go yet, across an area of the Atlantic notorious for its midsummer highs and their calms. With no engine.

I close the engine compartment and finish wiping off my hands and arms. I put on the kettle.

Within minutes Barbara is drying the last of her tears, reassuring me now.

'I'm okay.'

'I know you are.'

I've had time to sift through our options. I am ready when she asks, 'Where are you?'

'Bummed out, just like you. As weird as it sounds, I'm

also intrigued that we get a chance to sail our way in – no engine – just like those guys did for a thousand years.'

Barbara focuses on her tea, only later admitting, 'I'm intrigued, too.'

During a mid-morning radio exchange with a concerned friend, she has recovered completely. 'We have all the food and water we need. We have a great boat. And the girls are treating this like a camp-out.

'We're going to be fine.'

Katie and Erin take their reading from us during lunch. The honest language of the eyes. Like us, they are tired and disappointed. They are also resilient, and caught up in the drama of our situation. They are getting in touch with the toughness beneath their exuberant girlishness, the physical confidence called out in this real-time family adventure.

'A walk in the park,' Katie winks at me, drawing on daddy talk.

In time our discussion shifts to the practical challenges we face. The loss of the engine means an end to the luxuries that easy energy provides. Our refrigerated food will spoil within 36 hours. We cannot run the desalinator to upgrade our water supplies.

We will save the remainder of our precious electrical reserves for a single halogen light below, and only the most essential weather reports on the radio. Barbara will shorten her cherished radio contacts with other sailors in transit, deepening the isolation we all feel.

We spend most of the next two days becalmed. I quietly fight to stay sane. Where are those monkish reserves?

'Let's make the most of it,' Barbara reminds me.

'It's great for getting things aired out and dried.' Boat school goes into high gear on days when we are not dogged by swells.

When the wind finally arrives, it comes dead out of the East.

'Go figure,' even Barbara has limits.

It comes with a vengeance. A series of lows have parked west of the Azores, crowding out the mythical Azores high. They spin off Easterly, Northeasterly and Southeasterly winds that are right in the face. We tack and tack and tack again, working for every mile we make. We are getting our brains beaten out.

We juke to the North, making our way up to 41° latitude, looking in vain for a North wind to provide us with relief. The relentless, close-hauled sailing is taking a toll on our sails, in spite of our efforts to keep them from luffing. The sound of it, the incessant rattle and snap, wears on my increasingly frazzled state of mind.

It doesn't help to hear the mayhem the winds are wreaking on boats to the South. A German single-hander has burned up an autopilot, hundreds of miles from the Azores. Some Canadian friends try to stay upbeat after their main blows apart and their windvane breaks. The weariness in their voices echoes our own. These lows are taking no prisoners.

The ocean provides. Dolphins show up at 3am, intent on some early morning antics. I am sprawled on the foredeck, in a tangle of sails and sheets, flirting with self-pity. *It's all a game*, they seem to say, and I want to agree.

'We made them ourselves,' the girls announce in the morning, a bright-eyed procession up into the cockpit with

Father's Day cards and cupcakes laced with M&Ms. Their spirits elevate, as do day-long thoughts of their brother. The wind enters the spirit of the day, on the beam now, a long-awaited acceleration.

'Less than three hundred miles to Horta,' Barbara announces, GPS in hand.

Erin goes quiet and pale as the shadows deepen, an anguished 'I'm sorry, Daddy' when she throws up on me.

● ● ● ● ●

THE MARCH TO HORTA STALLS THE next evening, the casualty of waning winds. The mast head wind indicator spins aimlessly, the sails flog towards delirium. The wind dies altogether just after dawn. I drop the sails and go below, easing myself into our berth.

'I've met my match,' to a surprised and drowsy Barbara.

A mid-morning breeze calls me back to the wheel. We ghost in the direction of Horta. By afternoon we have twelve fresh knots, and the first of many island birds.

Our batteries are almost depleted now. We are into jerry can reserves for water. The lithium battery on our GPS is gone, its memory and waypoints vanished. But we do have a freshening breeze, and the energy that comes with it. The girls are irrepressible over dinner, excited about the inevitable landfall. They drag their weary parents along.

Seated in the cockpit after dark, soothed by a steady breeze, I juggle the mixed feelings I often experience at the end of a long passage. I can't wait for the feel of solid land, the hot shower, the cheeseburger and beer. I look forward to swapping stories with other sailors, elbows up on a cafe table. I also feel a low-grade melancholy. This stage of the journey is ending. As harsh and exhausting as it is, every extended passage stands on its own, beauty and isolation.

No shoreside equivalent that I know of.

A squall sweeps in unannounced, yanking me out of reverie. *Grace* lunges over on her side, hostage of a full set of sails. I try to find a point of sail that will spill some wind off the sails. They explode in protest when I turn into the gusts, rattling towards destruction by luffing. Barbara bolts up into the cockpit.

'Take the wheel. Keep us just off the wind.'

I lurch awkwardly up onto the deck and fight to keep my balance as I stagger to the mast. 'Got to get these sails down,' to the stirring in my chest. The main first, hand-over-hand, yanking it down, out of the reach of the howling wind. I leave it wallowing on the deck and dive back to the cockpit to furl in the genny.

'Come on, come on,' a stirring in my chest.

'Keep it on the wind,' I shout when Barbara steps towards me from the helm. 'I can do this.'

But I can't.

I am struggling by the time I reach the mast again, the heft in my chest. I uncleat the halyard – *breathe* – and release it.

I move to the foredeck next, and begin pulling the genny out of the water. One arm is going numb as I yank. I let go of the sail and sprawl backwards, away from the brink, onto a bundle of sail on the deck. I fumble for the bottle of nitro in my pocket, get one under my tongue, then a second. *Keep breathing. Let go.*

Off in the distance, Barbara is shouting.

'Are you okay?'

I try to yell my okayness.

She can't hear me. She is still shouting. The fear in her voice rolls up over me, out into the night. Getting louder as she comes. Standing over me now, down beside me.

'Are you okay?' Tears in her eyes, her hands on me.

'I will be,' trying not to dislodge the saving bitterness spreading out into my mouth.

•••••

HOURS LATER, AFTER WE HAVE BUNDLED THE SAILS into crude piles, and lashed them to the deck; after we have sorted the tangle of halyards and sheets, laughed scornfully at the ensuing calm, the vacuum behind the squall, and staggered down below; after we have stripped away the foul-weather gear, the wettest of our clothes and crawled into our berth and are holding each other, Barbara starts to cry.

'You scared me.'

She is sobbing now, convulsing, the surge of fear too long contained, coughing, retching, the rancid price of bravery.

I say nothing – this is her ache – only hold her.

•••••

A MURMUR, A STIR IN THE damp air below, the first lapping on the hull.

'I think we've got a breeze.'

I roll over and sit up on the edge of the berth. I look down the length of the boat, out into the cockpit. The flag is fluttering at the stern.

I pull on some clothes.

The breeze is freshening when I reach the cockpit, the sun working its way through the haze. I feel better when the sails are up. We are underway again. Horta awaits.

The North wind stays with us through the day and into the night. It is hard not to get caught up in the girls' excitement about the pizza and ice cream they will devour, the pure pleasure of walking on solid ground.

An ominous, grinding sound rousts me out of late-afternoon complacency, then the first of several hearty thumps. A glance over the transom confirms my worst fears. The windvane is lurching erratically behind the boat. Two of its four lashings have given way simultaneously. The most reliable helmsperson is overboard, tangled in the water generator line.

By the time we work it free and hoist it aboard, the wind is up again and gusting. We shorten the foresail and double reef the main. If we are lucky, we can make an engineless entry to Horta in the next twenty-four hours. Without a windvane, one of us will have to be at the wheel for the duration.

'Piece of cake,' I wink at Barbara. A grin works its way up through her grimace. We are okay, but we are tired.

As if on cue, we get our most brilliant sunset of the passage, an extravaganza that has Katie saying, 'Dad, close your mouth.' Later, after the lights are out below, an almost full moon emerges from its week-long cloister in the clouds. It ushers me into stillness, beyond calculation and contraction, beyond any need for reprieve.

●●●●●

THE FIRST FAINT OUTLINES OF Faial and Pica penetrate the horizon before noon. A chorus of 'land ho, land ho!' from Erin, her hands above her head, a staccato of barefoot high-stepping. By dusk we are ghosting down alongside the cliffs and the volcanic outcroppings of Faial. Midnight finds us fighting our way through the current that funnels down between Faial and Pica, in dying and contrary breezes. On our second attempt, we glide in behind the massive sea wall at Horta. We drop anchor by 1am.

After a late-night bowl of soup, Barbara and I retreat to the cockpit. We pour and hoist two ceremonial cups of Baileys.

'Good for you, girl.'

'We did it,' leaning with warm weariness into me.

'Wasn't always pretty, but we did.'

It is the moon's turn to witness, and the unflinching eye of the crater above the town.

●●●●●

DAYS OF REPAIR AND REUNION: sails to stitch, a windvane to remount, the obstreperous engine to fix. We lounge for long afternoons and evenings with that floating community of long-distance cruisers. Every one of us has paid our dues. Embellished, almost Irish tales are floated, the beginnings of myth, to long rolling shoreside swells of laughter.

Katie and Erin marshal a hoard of equally high-spirited friends. Working in tag-teams, they transform *Grace* into a fifty-foot playground, overwhelming our lame attempts to maintain order. The boats off which we are rafted are mostly good-natured about this pony-legged invasion, the patter of bare feet from early morning to night.

We sleep soundly through long, watchless nights, *Grace* securely tethered. We rest enough to dip down into that deeper exhaustion which underlies, residue of a difficult passage. Morning finds us moving in slow motion. There is a massive pile of laundry to do on a day whose sunny skies hold the possibility of a quick-drying session. Cushions to air out, all the wetness that accumulates in weeks at sea.

Life settles into that delicious rhythm of warmth, work and conversation that is the staple of a cruiser's life. We ingest ample amounts of low-priced bread and cheese, plastic glasses topped off with inexpensive Portuguese wine. We quickly replace pounds lost at sea, needed or not. Future destinations inevitably work their way into conversation, early reminders that the flotilla, boat-by-boat, will soon be moving on.

A week into port life, a blustery front moves in. Rain drives the girls below for a long-overdue stint of boat school. I retreat with a faulty radio microphone to a shop in Horta. I later discover the umbrella-strewn balcony of a coffee shop overlooking the harbour. I scratch out a first disorganized account of our passage. Nothing I write seems adequate, faint impressions mostly.

Even this cursory glance calls up a cartoon in an English sailing magazine. Two old salts are clinging to the helm in a gale, rain gear pulled down across their faces in a vain attempt to protect themselves from the spray blown off towering waves. Gasping for breath in the deepening storm, one shouts to the other, 'I just can't understand what those chaps see in golf!'

To an outside observer, it must be hard to understand

what calls cruisers to the sea, leaning into the wind, storm after calm after crisis, the physical and emotional over-extension. I think I know, but fumble for the words, scribbling and crossing out. The breakage and mishaps are easiest to capture – stark, graphic, unromantic.

It is that other reality, however, experienced differently by each of us, that makes the heart race, draws us out again. Experience as intense as words are inadequate. Life in that last bluewater wilderness. The residual glitter of a school of flying fish, making their escape across the bow of the boat. The extravagant mayhem of a great storm, and what the sun does when the clouds finally part. The vacuous eye of a squid left on the deck by a breaking wave. The curious surprise of a sea turtle, the inscrutable glimpse of a surfacing whale.

I am here because it is, quite simply, the most vivid and immense and beautiful and terrible place I know. The place where I am most awake, smallest, and most whole.

• • • • •

GRAVEYARD SHIFT IN THE ATLANTIC, eight hundred miles from the promise of Ireland. We are making our way under a forgiving moon, at the far edge of an overdue Azores high. I am awash in after-images of Horta, firmly entrenched this time, flower-strewn and drenched in history. Stop-over point for Columbus and Slocum, she now entertains hundreds of Atlantic passage-makers each summer. None is more vivid than Charlie Pfeffer.

Charlie first pops up on a radio net shortly out of Bermuda. A seasoned Maine sailor, he has cruised into early retirement. He is making a belated run at the Atlantic in his Shannon 38, *Piper*, single-handing to the Azores with his beloved terrier, Ollie. Charlie confides that he is not entirely sure about Ollie's sea stomach. Apparently there have been several 'accidents' since leaving Bermuda.

Charlie and I talk briefly when water damage behind a circuit panel threatens his entire electrical system. When I ask him if he is okay, he sounds surprised by the question, answering with stoical New England assurance that he is fine.

For the next couple of weeks, Charlie is an engaging voice over the radio. He regales listeners with a string of limericks about his passage. He laces Ollie's adventures into many conversations. By the time we reach Horta, he and Ollie are already minor celebrities among sailors who frequent the net.

Charlie does not disappoint in person. He has a red face and white hair and more than a little mischief in his eyes. We first meet on a breakwater near his rafted boat. He is moving across the last boat before the seawall, a sail bag on his shoulder. I stop to give him a hand. In the ensuing conversation, we discuss his crossing and ours. Our leaky fuel injector comes up. He has a complete set of spare injectors for the same model engine. He offers one to me, which I agree to buy.

We talk regularly over the next few days. For a New England sailor, he can get pretty animated. He is ecstatic about being reunited with his wife, Deborah, recently arrived from the States. Their affection for each other is evident when I meet her later.

Charlie is equally animated when talking about the cruising life. He has been sailing the East Coast for years, but always on a leash. He can hardly contain his excitement about cruising Europe. Open horizons, after all these years.

'Somebody told me you singlehanded the Atlantic,' he opens one afternoon.

We spend the better part of an hour comparing notes. Any semblance of reserve is set aside. Although he won't say it out loud, it is clear that he is proud of his recent passage, just he and Ollie. Every sailor's dream, out there alone.

'I also heard you've had a run of heart problems.'

As Deborah prepares dinner in the galley below, we swap stories of cardiac misadventure. Charlie had an angioplasty six years ago.

'No problems since then.'

We talk about the risks and benefits of sailing with a bad heart, concluding, of course, that the benefits outweigh the risks.

'What better excuse can you have for being out here,' Charlie leans in, 'than not knowing how long you're going to live?'

'Exactly.' We lean back, chuckling, elbows out over the lifelines. It seems so simple.

An informal rally is arranged for the weekend, an overnight jaunt to a nearby island. Katie and Erin are having too much shore fun for Barbara and me to break away. Charlie is up early, making last-minute preparations. Without the benefit of a common language, he and Deborah have invited a local Portuguese couple to join them for the 'big race.' He greets them when they arrive. A few minutes later he excuses himself and goes down the companionway to the galley. He stops there, turns awkwardly, and falls over, unconscious.

In spite of emergency treatment from two doctors at the dock, and later at the local hospital, Charlie never regains consciousness. He is dead at 55, felled by the 'bad heart' we had shrugged off two days earlier.

Barbara and I stare at each other when word comes back that Charlie is gone. I finally look away, unable to maintain the gaze.

'Damn.' Barbara reaches out and touches my arm.

We pour our energy into taking care of the girls. This is a new, unwanted reality for them. We stay close to each other throughout the day and into the night. We walk hand-in-hand, almost everywhere we go.

The shocked cruising community closes in around Deborah in a show of attention that might seem overdone to an outsider. We are also helping ourselves. Charlie has got under everyone's skin in a short, intense time. Two of Charlie and Deborah's sons, Richard and Eric, arrive on the first flight they can book. They discover the instant intimacy that bonds long-distance cruisers. Arrangements are made, long hours spent in an ongoing, informal wake. An evening vigil is convened around a commemorative heart painted on the seawall. Every anchor light in the harbour burns in his honour. Every one but Charlie and Deborah's *Piper*, her travelling tricolour aglow. Charlie is underway again.

• • • • •

WE ARE UNDERWAY ALSO, three days closer to the Ireland of my dreams. I go below to kiss everyone goodnight, grabbing a handful of vanilla wafers on my way back to the cockpit.

'We've got a blow coming,' Barbara warns evenly. 'We probably ought to get some reefs in before I bunk out.'

When the last light goes out a short time later, I am alone with the swelling intensity of the night, the avalanche of clouds running in from the Northwest. The temperature plummets. I don a woollen cap and gloves. These last days have been almost too easy. Tonight we get dusted.

Grace accelerates into the darkness, the easy power of a staysail and a double-reefed main. It reminds me of the occasional bluster on the way to the Azores, Charlie out there, making his way. How different to do it alone. This time I have the steady certainty that my family is sleeping below. However brutal the conditions, reinforcements are coming, usually armed with a cup of something hot.

Beyond the responsibility of it, there is also the fortified sense of *having* to survive, the agreeable burden of being needed. A knowledge I have sailed with on other dark nights, across seas that anticipated this one. Across that other wide ocean a decade ago, weary and alone, called home by Barbara and the kids.

Across the ocean of this aching heart.

My thoughts drift back to Charlie, and then to the stultifying rumour we heard over the single sideband earlier this evening. Talk of a boat found adrift between Bermuda and the Azores, a single deceased sailor aboard.

I scan the horizon for signs of life. For a while I am the survivor.

●●●●●

THE NEXT SEVERAL DAYS GIVE us a primer on North Atlantic sailing. A steady fare of twenty knots, and squalls that run up higher. *Grace* takes it like a thoroughbred, knifing through the irregular swell on a sustained tear towards Ireland. She makes short work of five hundred miles that can easily take a week when the Northeasterlies blow.

Life down below is an athletic event. Barbara marshals the girls through boat school and the other creative ventures they can manage. She keeps food coming out of the galley with an agility I cannot fathom, then finds the energy for long, graveyard watches. Katie and Erin are becoming seasoned sailors as well. They have almost entirely overcome the seasickness that bothered them early on. Taking their mother's lead, they put in for deck work, sail trim, and wheel time.

All of us are buttressed by the accumulating sea time. We are veterans now. Storms are part of who we are, discomfort and survivability. *Grace* has our full confidence. She has taken us to places we only read about before, and found the fair breeze hidden within the clouds. We still get tired, cranky, and discouraged, but it is getting harder to maintain fear for any long stretch.

The ocean is teaching us to deal with what is given, to draw on what is within.

On the morning of our eighth day out, the sky clears. The sun glistens on the salt-caked deck. The wind drops back to a mild 15 knots.

'We're getting there, Irish,' Barbara looks up from the GPS. 'Tomorrow morning, if we're lucky.'

I have made my way through Leon Uris's *Trinity* during our crossing. He has stoked the home fires thoroughly.

We are the first of our family to return to the Ireland my mother's people fled two generations ago. They left in coffin boats, equal parts hope and despair. We return now on *Grace*'s broad back, worn and wind-chafed and full of anticipation.

• • • • •

OUR LAST SUNSET AT SEA, a thousand shades of purple in the West. Then night itself, the silver moon an alchemist.

Everything is draped in silver now, my hands on the wheel, *Grace* with her sails and shrouds, the wave-tipped ocean spreading out in every direction. It would drape the wind in silver if it could. And these eyes, the eyes of a million sea creatures, all see what the moon has done, celebrate what the moon has done.

Beauty calls you out beyond the contracted self, invites immersion in the larger, unseen self. On this silver night, she whispers,

Wake up, John.
Wake up.

• • • • •

IRELAND DOES NOT DISAPPOINT. She rises lush and green out of the receding haze to the Northeast in the last week of July. Awash in the emotional equivalent of Blarney, I wipe away tears as we glide by the bluffs at Mizzenhead, pass Fastnet Rock to starboard. When the wind dies in the early afternoon, I reach down to start the engine. The thrice-cursed starter has deserted us again. None of the old tricks work.

'It figures,' Barbara exhales.

'It's perfect,' I counter.

In the late afternoon, on the beginnings of a breeze, we creep through the rocky entrance into the lush abundance of Schull Harbour. We drop our sails, then the anchor.

'You're home, Sweetheart.' Barbara moves up the deck towards me, arms open.

'Already was,' my arms around her.

'Always already am.'

Epilogue

'The real voyage of discovery consists not in seeking new landscapes, but in having new eyes.'

–Marcel Proust

I NO LONGER HAVE illusions of longevity. I would like to live long enough to see our son fully spread his wings, our daughters emerge from the sweet cocoon of childhood.

Nor is my death a likely mystery. The unsustainable ache in my chest, slipping below the waves into that larger, unimagined life.

What is left to me is that great storm – flowing through each of us – which is life itself. Dense, unthinkably light. Most of all, brief.

How I live it is what I have. Scant excuse for dallying at the edges.

My history as a dervish aside, life is richest when I slow it down to that place where the elemental intensity takes over. When the music stops, or is only music. When it is all slow motion, the power of a single second so obvious that you can hardly draw a breath.

The incandescence of a glance, a touch, a quality of light or dark, a leaf in the street.

And you realize all the motion is both a denial of life and a protection from the immensity of even one moment fully experienced.

I live in this only and abundant moment.

About the author and crew

JOHN OTTERBACHER AND HIS family lived on *Grace* for another five years, crossing the Atlantic four times and visiting over twenty countries on four continents.

They recently returned to Michigan so that Katie and Erin could finish their education.

John Ryan has finished graduate school, and is teaching and making films in Chicago.

Katie, who sailed across the Pacific during the summer after high school, attends college in Michigan.

Erin is a junior in high school, where she aspires to everything, all the time.

Barbara has returned to legal education and practice.

John divides his time between writing, speaking, consulting with clients, and walking the family dog, Chauncey.

Barbara and John are planning another extended cruise on *Grace*.

Acknowledgements

ALL MY LIFE I have been standing on the shoulders of generous others, appearing taller than I actually am. *Outrageous Grace* is no exception.

Each of the people listed below made a contribution – both to the book and to the lives within the book. I am giving their names in no particular order, with apologies to anyone I miss. I am grateful to each of them.

Dr Rick McNamara, Dan Hendrickson and Dr Colleen Tallen, Barry Johnson and Dana Wilcox, David and Paula Doyle, Bill Craft and Mary Padget, Tom Osbourne, Darcy Maxim, Tony and JenAnne Mance, Jan Meadowcroft, Andy and Nancy Robel, Bob and Deb VanderMolen, Janet Murphy, Liz Piercy, Reinder VanTil, Dan Gerber, Jim Harrison, Herb McCormick, Bernadette Bernon, Elaine Lembo, John Burnham, Paul Gelder, Tim Murphy, Kathy Gregory, Dr Jon Gans, Dick Holm, Carl Allore, Barb Cribar, Chris Komor, Trystan Lindquist, Bob and Gerri Williams, Kirsten Sloan, Johanna Deurling, Mary Osbourne, Russ Zimlich, Ann Dunham and Terry Hunefeld, Amy Kransteuber, David and Phyllis Oakes, Ruth Stevens and Tom Stellard, Patrick Foley, Tom Rademacher, Rich Deros, Gordon Olsen, Larry TenHarmsel,

Dominick Abel, Rev Bob Bonnot, Jonathan Collins, Peter Forthmann, John Golden, Roland Adam, Shannon Hager, Christine St John, Bob Bishop, Elwin Ruehs and Mary McGee, John Banks, Vonda Schmid and Noralee Potts of The Composing Room of Michigan, Willem Mineur, and Sam and Sara Speigel.

A special thanks to Judd Arnett and Rev Duncan Littlefair who poked and prodded and encouraged me, then took their leave before I finished the book. And to Cathy Weisbeck, Kim Hayslip, Angie Morse, Kate Hartson, Ric Miller and John Liskey, who have done the heavy lifting all along.

I would like to thank my brother, Jim, my sister Diane Osbourne, and Barb's sister, Audrey Craft, without whom our trip would not have been possible. And finally, my father and mother, John Otterbacher and Dena Dunn, who gave me much and travel with me everywhere.

Outrageous Grace belongs to each of you.

Glossary of Nautical Terms

alternator: an engine-mounted machine for generating electricity

backstay: a mast-supporting cable from the stern to the top of the mast

beam: the widest part of the boat

berth: a bed on a boat

boom: a sail-supporting spar running at right angles to the mast

boom vang: a line securing the boom to the toerail

bosun's chair: a halyard-supported seat used to lift someone up the mast

bow: the front end of a boat

bulkhead: a wall in the living area below decks

cabin sole: cabin floors

cam cleat: a spring-loaded clamp for securing a line

close-hauled: sailing towards the wind

cleat: a fitting around which a line is secured

coaming: splashboard on the deck, to keep water out of the cockpit

cradle: the framework on which a boat rests when out of the water

cutter:	a sailboat with two headsails forward of a single mast
desalinator:	a machine for removing salt from the water
drogue:	a sea anchor used to slow a boat's speed
EPIRB:	an electronic device which relays a boat's position to rescue a vessel
foresail:	the most forward sail on a boat
forestay:	a mast-supporting cable strung between the bow and the top of the mast
furl:	to roll up a sail, shortening it in the process
galley:	a boat's kitchen
gangplank:	a mobile plank usually with projecting cross pieces fixed to it, serving as a gangway for a boat
genoa:	a large foresail, also known as a 'genny'
GPS:	an electronic device which tells the boat's position
halyard:	a line used to hoist sails
head:	the toilet on a boat
helm:	the tiller or wheel that controls the rudder
jackline:	a line running lengthwise to which safety harnesses are secured
jerry can:	a narrow, flat-sided container for water or fuel
jib:	a triangular sail forward of the mast
jibe:	to turn by getting the wind onto the opposite side of the mainsail
keel:	the fore-aft blade on the bottom of the hull
knot:	a nautical mile, about 1.15 of a statute mile
lazy jacks:	lines from the topping lift to the boom which make it easier to control dropped sails

lifeline:	a line rigged around the deck to prevent people from falling overboard
luff:	flapping at the edge of a sail
mainsail:	the large sail aft of the mast, also known as the 'main'
pilot chart:	ocean charts which give monthly averages for wind speed and direction, wave height, etc.
reef:	to reduce the area of a sail in a strong wind
rhumbline:	the course followed by a boat sailing in a fixed direction
rig:	the mast and its supporting shrouds and stays
samson post:	a strong post on the foredeck
satnav:	a satellite navigational device that gives a boat's position
sextant:	a mechanical instrument used to determine a boat's position
shackle:	a looped metal fitting that secures the end of a line to something
sheet:	a line used to trim a sail
single hand:	to sail a boat alone
single sideband:	a high frequency, long-distance two-way radio
shroud:	mast-supporting cables, strung from the sides of the boat to the top of the mast
spinnaker:	a large, balloon-shaped foresail for use in very high wind
spreader:	arms off the mast that extend out to the shrouds

starboard: the right side of the boat

staysail: a triangular-shaped headsail, secured to a stay

stern: the back end of a boat

sump pump: a pump used to remove water from within the boat

transom: the flat-back surface of a boat

winch: a mechanical drum around which lines are wound to draw them in

windlass: a machine used to haul up anchor chain or rope

windvane: a mechanical device which uses the wind to steer the boat

A Final Note to the Reader

I suspect I was born with a book under my arm. Long before I could travel outside of the neighbourhood, books took me far afield, introducing me to adventure and the world. I often dreamed about sitting down with the authors who wrote them, to ask questions and compare notes.

Sailing Grace, which I self-published in the USA in 2008, and this international edition titled *Outrageous Grace* (Adlard Coles Nautical, London), is my first book. I would love to hear what you think of it. I am not fishing for compliments. I am very interested in what the book calls up in you. Although I am very protective of my time and privacy, I would like to be available where I can. With that in mind, I am agreeing to select consultations and speaking engagements.

Go to www.sailing-grace.com to access pictures taken of our family during the period covered in the book and information about presentations, critical reviews and other opportunities. You can also sign up for regular email updates on the book, the crew and upcoming events.

About the Author

When John Otterbacher talks about 'living out beyond your fears', he is speaking from experience.

He grew up in the working class neighbourhoods of Grand Rapids, Michigan, paying for college with a series of factory and construction jobs. After earning his doctorate in clinical psychology, he taught at college and served as a state representative and senator. During his eight years in the legislature, John was a firebrand on health issues, leading successful fights for, among others, nursing home reform and the development of a statewide emergency medical service system.

John then returned to private practice, spending a decade providing consultation to individuals and organizations. In the mid-1980s, he took up sailing, spending three years 'learning' in the Great Lakes. He and his wife Barbara then took their children, John Ryan (13) and Katie (8 months) on a fifteen month cruise to the Mediterranean and the Caribbean. During this period, he also sailed single-handed across the Atlantic.

In 1998, John and Barbara did an extended cruise with their girls (Katie, 9, and Erin, 5), spending the next six

244 ✧ OUTRAGEOUS GRACE

years sailing the Atlantic (four crossings), the North Sea, the Baltic, the Mediterranean, and the Caribbean.

John currently lives and writes in Michigan.

Outrageous Grace is the international edition of his first book, *Sailing Grace*.

www.sailing-grace.com